EMBROIDERY SAMPLER COLLECTIVE

18 Designs • 75+ Stitches • 12 Artists • Endless Inspiration

By C&T Publishing

Publisher: Amy Barrett-Daffin

Creative Director: Gailen Runge

Senior Editor: Roxane Cerda

Editors: Gailen Runge, Madison Moore

Cover/Book Designer: April Mostek

Production Coordinator: Zinnia Heinzmann

Illustrators: Aliza Shalit, and Kirstie Pettersen

Photography Coordinator: Rachel Ackley

Photography by C&T publishing, Inc., unless otherwise noted below:
Pages 6, 106, 109 by Stella Caraman
Pages 39 (top left), 110–121 by Aliaksandra Dzyachenka

Location for some lifestyle photography generously provided by Vinteige, a vintage furniture and decor store in Walnut Creek, California.

Published by Stash Books, an imprint of C&T Publishing, Inc., P.O. Box 1456, Lafayette, CA 94549

Library of Congress Cataloging-in-Publication Data

Names: C & T Publishing editor

Title: Embroidery sampler collective : 18 designs, 75+ stitches, 12 artists, endless inspiration / by C&T Publishing.

Description: Lafayette, CA : Stash Books, [2025] | Summary: Embroidery Sampler Collective brings together 12 amazing designers, offering 18 stunning embroidery samplers, and 75+ creative stitches to create embroidery projects that range from timelessly traditional to delightfully whimsical"-- Provided by publisher.

Identifiers: LCCN 2025026967 | ISBN 9781644036617 trade paperback | ISBN 9781644036624 ebook

Subjects: LCSH: Embroidery--Patterns

Classification: LCC TT771 .E48 2025 | DDC 746.44--dc23/eng/20250806

LC record available at https://lccn.loc.gov/2025026967

Printed in China

10 9 8 7 6 5 4 3 2 1

WELCOME TO THE EMBROIDERY SAMPLER DESIGN COLLECTIVE! We've brought together eighteen projects from twelve amazing designers so you can stitch, learn, and be inspired by endless ways to thrive as an embroidery artist.

Embroidery samplers are a great way to learn new stitches, represent the world around you in creative new ways, and get a taste for different embroidery styles. From stunning natural subjects by Aliaksandra Dzyachenka, Megan Zaniewski, and Melissa Galbraith to playful scenes by Anne Oliver, Carley Pettitt, Louise Waston, and Aimee Ray or classic decorations by Christen Brown, Laura Wasilowski, Jennifer Davidson, Stella Caraman, and Theresa Lawson—you will find a project to inspire and delight!

The projects are preceeded by a full stitch library that teaches more than 75 stitches step-by-step. It's an incredible resource for a huge variety of stitch shapes and textures, setting you up for a lifetime of creating embroidery art! Soon enough, you'll be working on a design for your own original sampler to display.

The stitch illustrations in the library are provided in large part courtesy of Christen Brown, author of *Hand Embroidery Dictionary*, *Embroidered & Embellished*, *Beaded Embroidery Stitching*, and *Beyond Crazy Quilts*, among other titles. Additionally, thank you to Judith Baker Montano, Aimee Ray, Jennifer Clouston, and Melissa Galbraith for providing instructions in the stitch library as noted on the legal page and within the chapter.

Happy Stitching!

CONTENTS

80
54
58
66
114
70
76
48
86
92
44
62
110
118

STITCHES

ALGERIAN EYE STITCH

This stitch is also known as the star eyelet stitch.

1. Come up at A and go down at B (the center of the stitch) with a straight stitch.

2. Come up at C and go down at B. Repeat the straight stitches around the shape, always inserting at B.

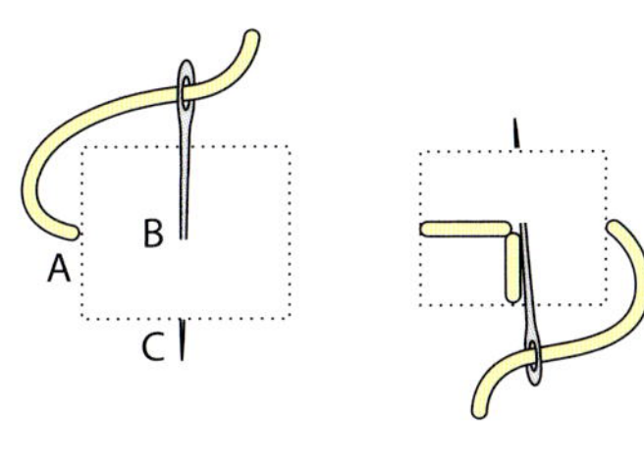

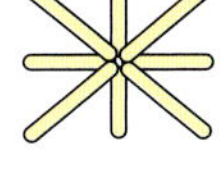

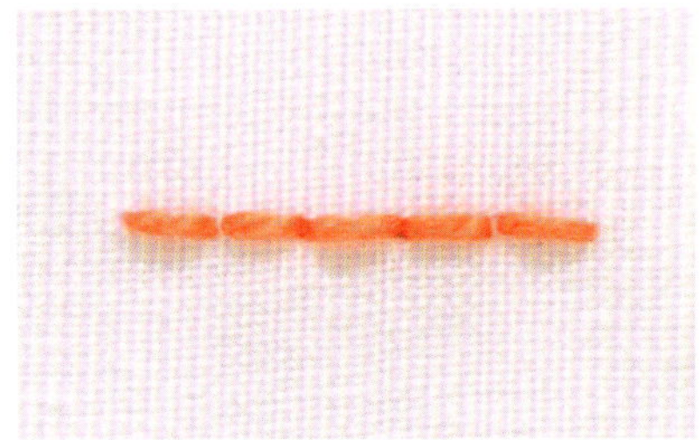

BACKSTITCH

1. Come up at A. *Backstitch the needle in one motion, down at B and up at C. Pull the needle through the fabric. C now becomes A.

2. Repeat from * to finish the row. To end the stitch, go down at B of the last stitch.

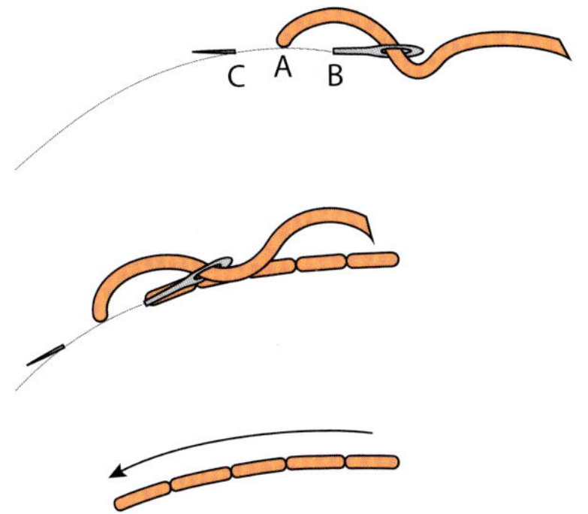

BASKET WEAVE STITCH

1. Create parallel stitches in a horizontal or vertical direction across the fabric.

2. Then using a new thread, weave stitches through the base stitches, alternating between going over and under each stitch.

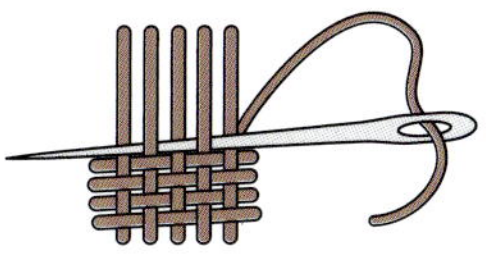

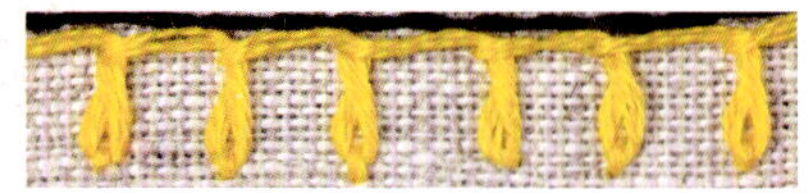

BASQUE STITCH

This stitch is worked between 2 horizontal lines.

1. Bring the thread out on the upper line at A. Move over slightly and bring the needle down at B and up at C, taking the thread across the needle, then looping the thread under the needle point.

2. Pull the needle through to form a twisted loop.

3. Insert the needle in at D to catch the loop and out at E.

4. Repeat Steps 1–3 a short distance away to form a row of stitches.

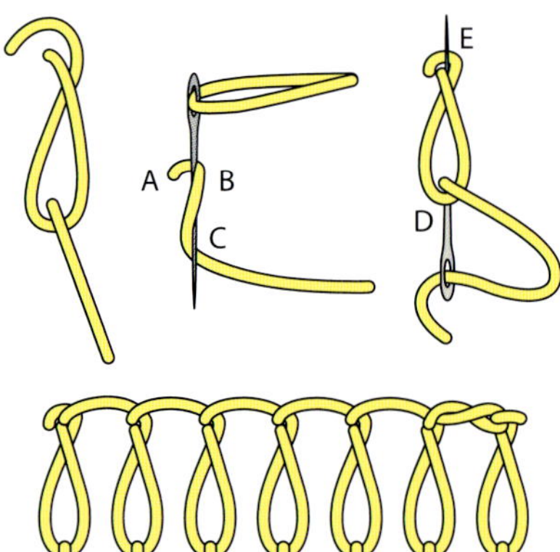

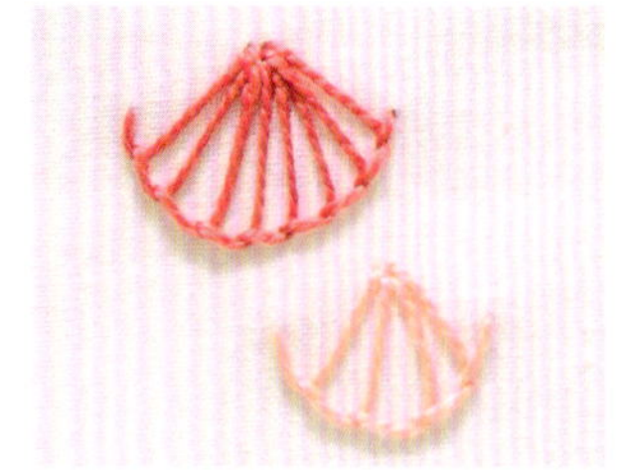

BELL FLOWER STITCH

1. Draw a half-circle and mark the center. Follow Step 1 of the blanket stitch (right), *with B as the center point and A and C on the curved line.

2. Repeat from *, working the stitches around the curve. To end the stitch, go down at D.

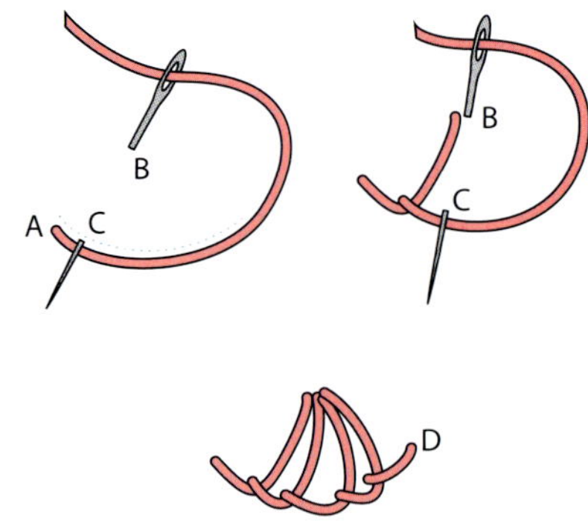

BLANKET STITCH

1. Come up at A. *In one motion, go down at B and up at C. Wrap the working thread under the tip of the needle. Pull the needle through the fabric.

2. Repeat from * to finish the row. To end the stitch, go down at D or a short distance away.

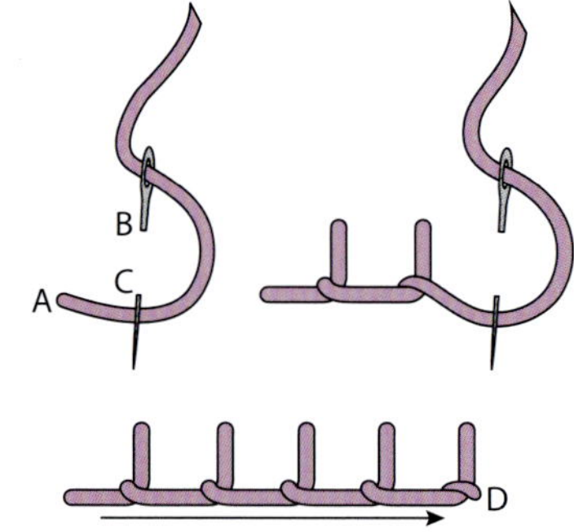

BLANKET STITCH LOOPED

1. Come up at A. *In one motion, go down at B and up at C. Wrap the working thread under the eye and the tip of the needle and back to the base of the stitch. Pull the needle through the fabric.

2. Go down at D to catch the loop. Come up at E.

3. Repeat from * to finish the stitch. To end the stitch, go down at F.

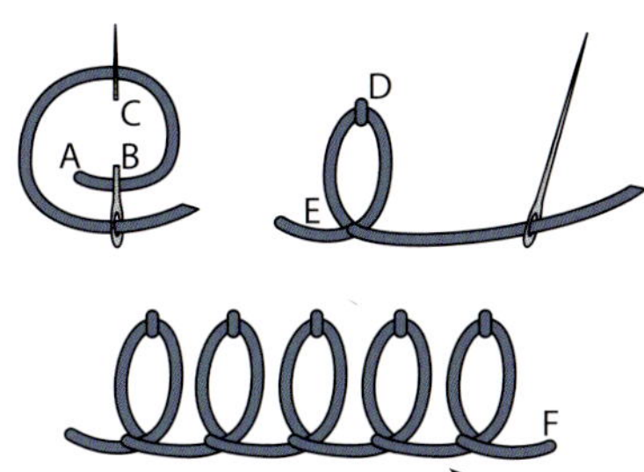

BLANKET STITCH WITH LOOSE KNOT STITCH

1. *Work 1 blanket stitch (page 8). Go under the base stitch only; wrap the working thread under the tip of the needle. Pull the thread firmly around the base stitch.

2. Repeat from * to finish the row. To end the stitch, go down at D.

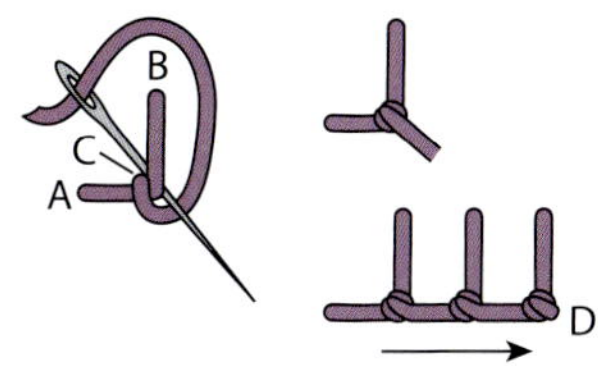

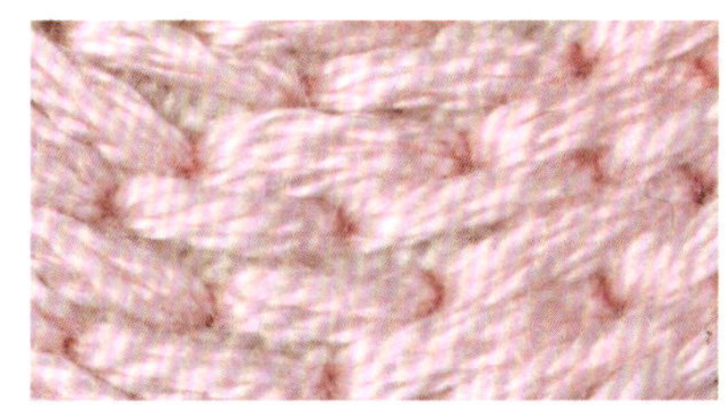

BRICK STITCH

Brick stitch is a backstitch worked in offset rows. This gives the appearance of a brick wall. It is great for filling in sections of a design and adding texture. See backstitch, page 7.

BULLION KNOT

1. Bring your needle through at A and put it back through a stitch length away at B. The length of the stitch is dependent on the size of your bullion knot.

2. Bring your needle out again at A, but do not pull your needle all the way through; instead, leave it halfway. Now start to wrap your thread around the tip of the needle. You may need to tilt the tip of the needle upward slightly to get these loops to stay on.

3. Wrap the thread around the needle five or six times so that the coil of thread will cover the length of stitch.

4. Place your thumb on the coiled thread and pull the needle through slowly and carefully so as not to disturb the coil. Insert the needle at B and gently pull the thread through until the bullion knot lies flat.

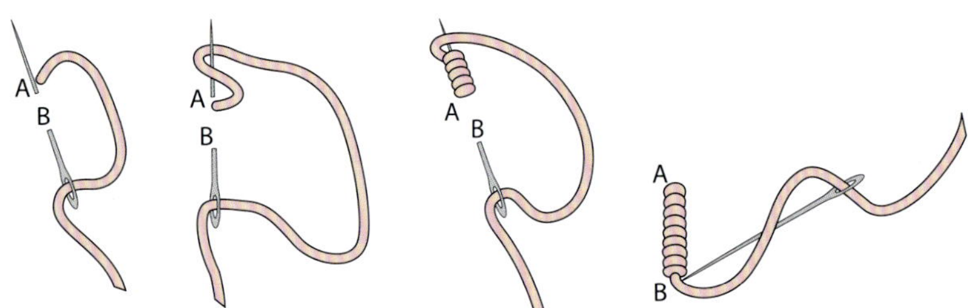

BUTTONHOLE WHEEL STITCH

This stitch is also known as the buttonhole circle stitch.

1. Draw a circle and mark the center point. Follow Step 1 of the blanket stitch (page 8), *with B as the center of the stitch and A and C on the curved line.

2. Repeat from *, working the stitches around the circle. To end the stitch, go down next to the first stitch.

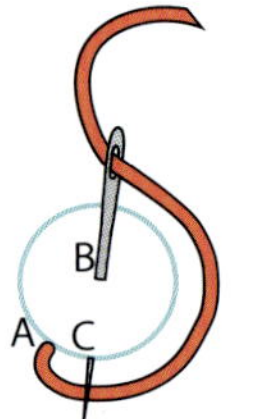

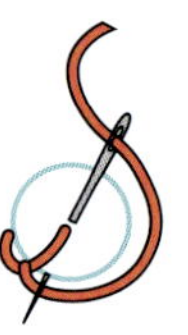

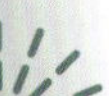

Stitch instructions from Jennifer Clouston's *Foolproof Flower Embroidery*, C&T Publishing.

CAST ON STITCH

1. Bring the needle to the surface of the work at A and pull the thread through.

2. Insert the needle at the desired length for the stitch at B and emerge at A. Do not pull the needle through.

3. Hold the thread with your left thumb and middle finger approximately 3″ (7.6cm) away from the surface of the work. Place your left index finger under the thread.

4. Rotate your left hand toward you in a clockwise direction and slip the loop off your index finger and onto the needle.

5. Pull the working thread toward you, sliding the knot down the needle onto the fabric.

6. Support the wraps on the needle with thumb and index finger and pull the needle through. Pull the thread away from and then towards you. Reinsert at B.

7. Take the needle through to the back of the work at B.

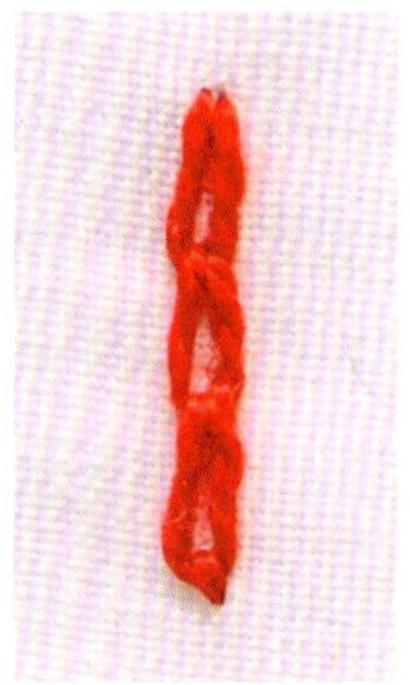

CHAIN STITCH

1. Come up at A. *In one motion, go down at B and up at C. Wrap the working thread under the tip of the needle. Pull the needle through the fabric.

2. Repeat from * to finish the row, starting inside the previous loop. To finish the stitch, go down at D.

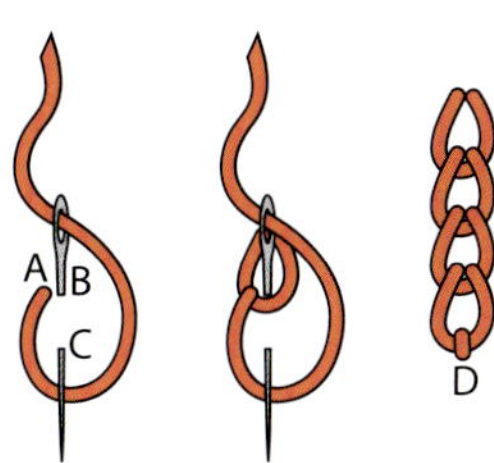

CHAIN STITCH CABLE

1. Come up at A. *Wrap the thread over the needle once.

2. In one motion, go down at B and up at C. Wrap the working thread under the tip of the needle, and pull the knot close to the fabric. Pull the thread through the fabric.

3. Repeat from * to finish the row. To end the stitch, go down at D.

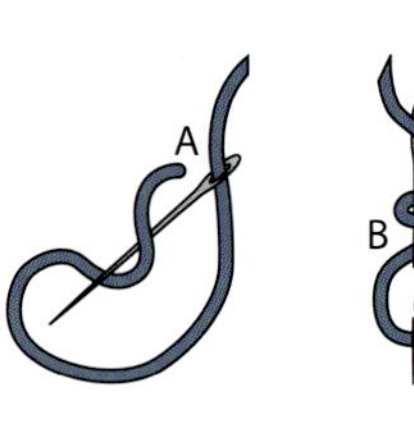

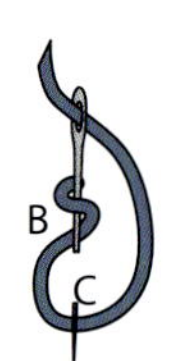

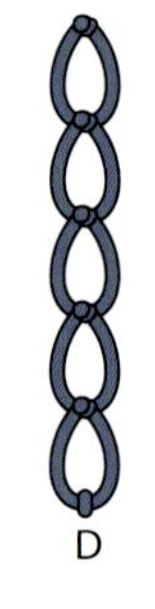

CHAIN STITCH DOUBLE

1. *Follow the directions for the chain stitch (page 11), working the stitch slightly angled from the seam.

2. In one motion, go down at D next to B and up at E on the seam.

3. To finish the row, repeat from *, beginning in the loop of the previous stitch. To end the stitch, go down at F.

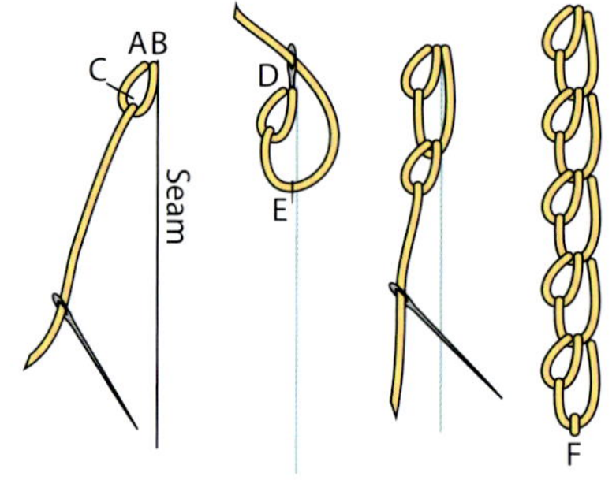

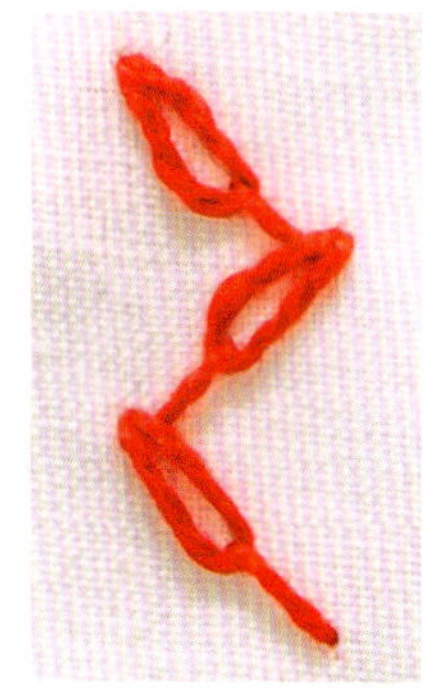

CHAIN STITCH FEATHERED

1. Follow Step 1 of the chain stitch (page 11), angling the stitch away from the seam. Go down at D, a short distance away.

2. Stitch the next stitch beginning at D of the previous stitch. Repeat Steps 1 and 2, angling the stitches from side to side.

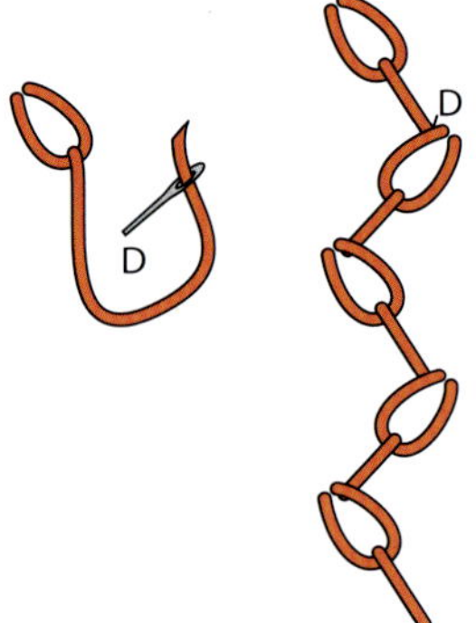

CHAIN STITCH OPEN

Work this stitch between 2 parallel lines.

1. Come up at A. *In one motion, go down at B and up at C. Pull the needle through the fabric, leaving a slight loop.

2. Repeat from * to finish the row, working B into the previous stitch. To end the stitch, go down at D. Come up at E and down at F.

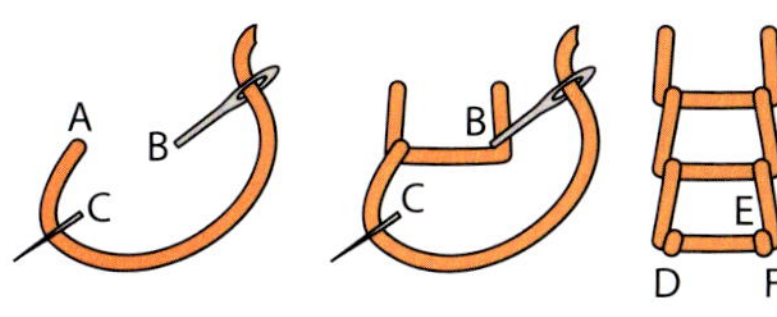

CHAIN STITCH TWISTED

1. Come up at A. *In one motion, go down at B and up at C. Wrap the working thread under the tip of the needle. Pull the needle through the fabric.

2. Repeat from * to finish the row. To end the stitch, go down at D.

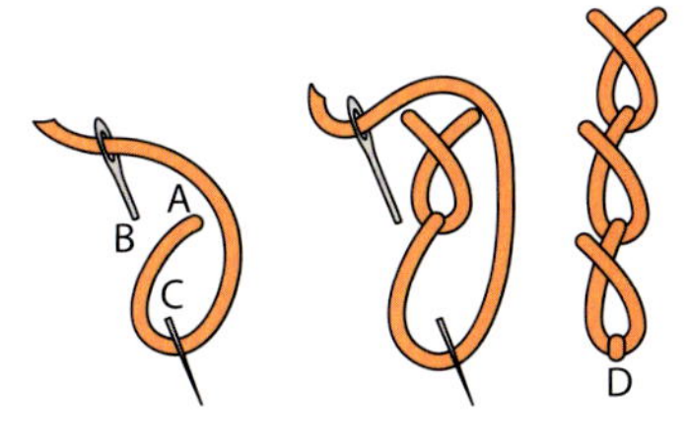

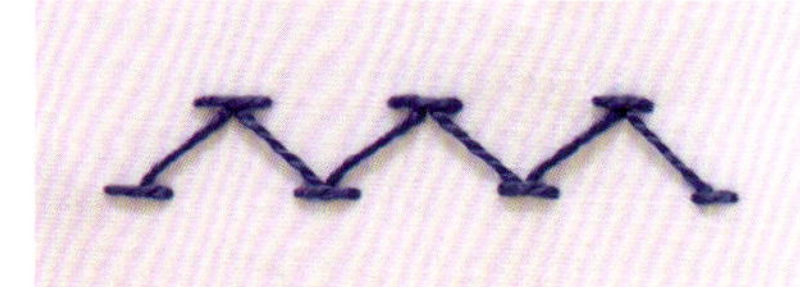

CHEVRON STITCH

Work this stitch between 2 horizontal lines.

1. Come up at A. Backstitch in one motion down at B and up at C. Pull the needle through the fabric.

2. Backstitch in one motion down at D and up at E. Pull the needle through the fabric. Backstitch in one motion down at F and up at D.

3. Repeat Step 2 to finish the row, alternating the stitches between the lines. To end the stitch, go down at F.

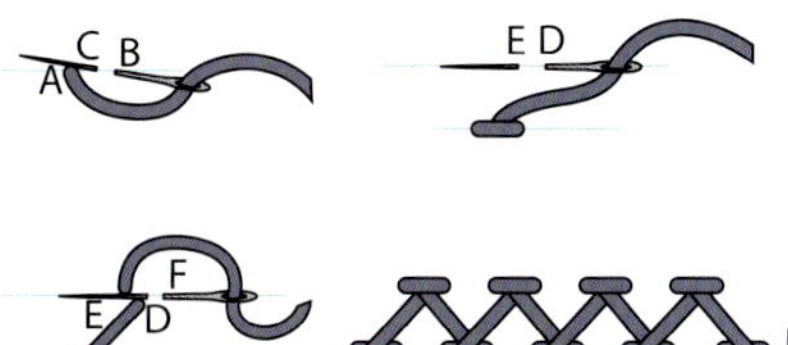

COLONIAL KNOT STITCH

1. Come up at A. Thread the needle under the loop close to A.

2. Wrap the working thread under the eye and the tip of the needle. Tighten the thread firmly.

3. Insert the needle into the fabric at B. Pull the thread through the loops.

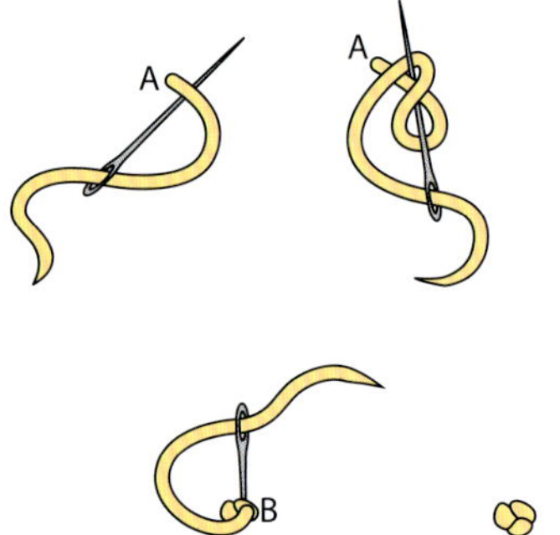

CONNECTED FLY STITCH

Draw a line to follow.

1. *Work 1 fly stitch with a long tail (page 19); the tail is the beginning of the next stitch, with D on the line. The last tail (from C to D) can be long or can be short to finish the row of stitches.

2. Repeat from * to finish the row.

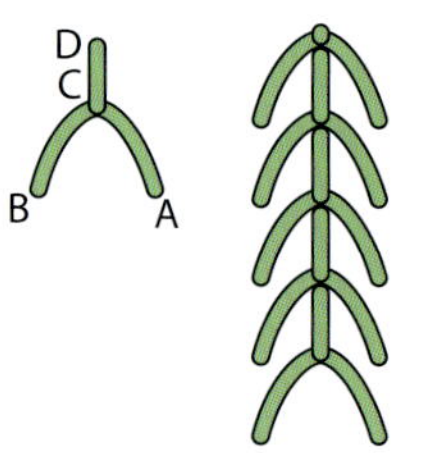

CORAL STITCH

1. Come up at A, hold the working thread straight. *In one motion, go down at B and up at C slightly angled. Wrap the working thread under the tip of the needle.

2. Pull the needle through the fabric to form a knot.

3. Repeat from * to finish the row. To end the stitch, go down at D a slight distance away from the last knot.

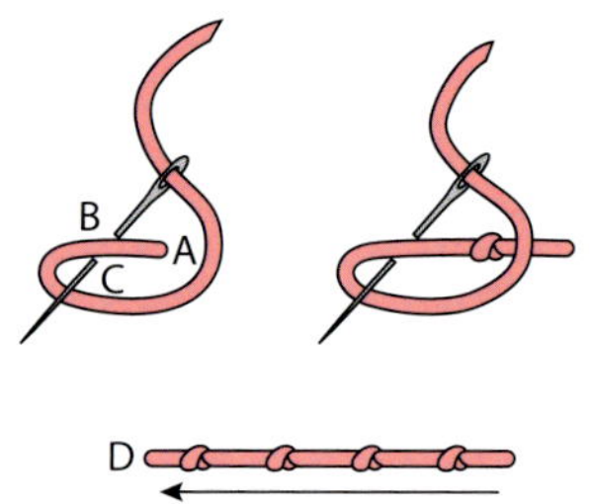

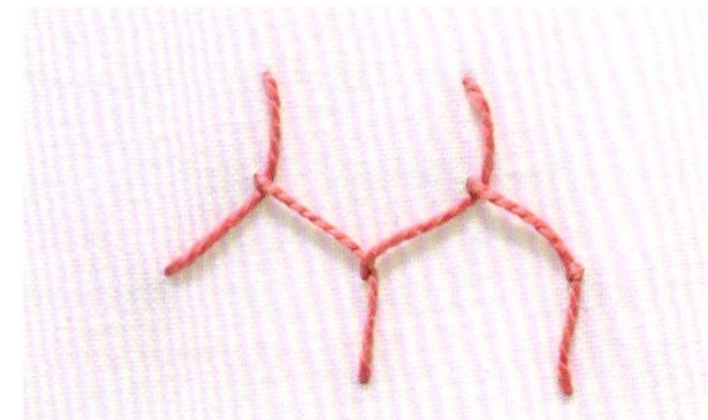

COUCH STITCH

1. Stitch a length of thread onto the fabric; knot and cut the end.

2. With a different color or type of thread, come up next to one end of the thread. Work straight stitches (page 35) across the row.

CRETAN STITCH

Work this stitch between 4 horizontal rows.

1. Come up at A on line 2. *In one motion, go down at B on line 4 and up at C on line 3. Wrap the working thread under the tip of the needle. Pull the needle through the fabric.

2. In one motion, go down at D on line 1 and up at E on line 2. Wrap the working thread under the tip of the needle. Pull the needle through the fabric.

3. Repeat from * to finish the row. To end the stitch, go down at F, either after Step 1 or Step 2.

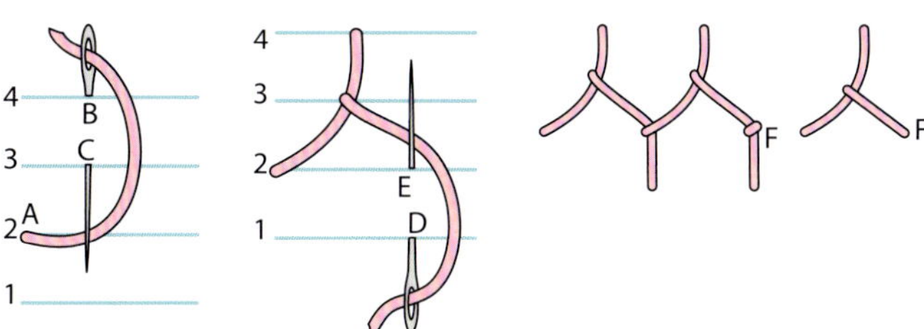

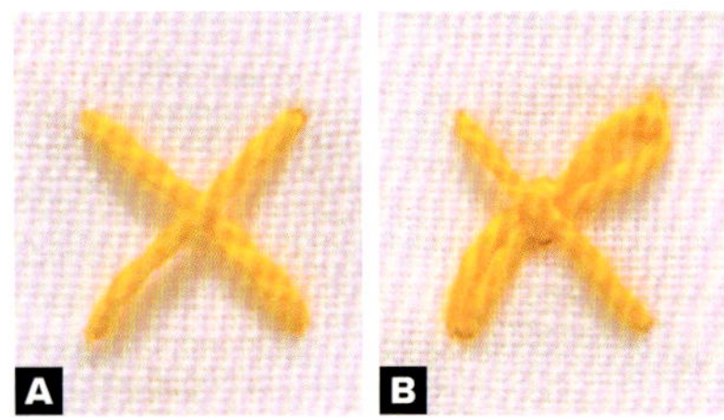

Stitch courtesy of Melissa Galbraith (see Designers, page 122)

A CROSS STITCH

1. Come up at A and go down at B.

2. Come up at C and go down at D, crossing over the first stitch.

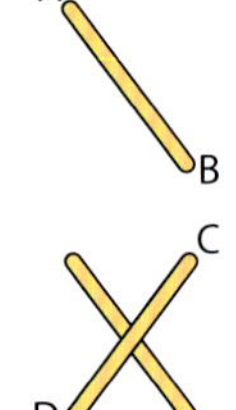

B CROSSED LAZY DAISY STITCH

1. Stitch 1 lazy daisy stitch (page 23).

2. Stitch 1 straight stitch (page 35) the same length and width, crossed over the first stitch.

3. Stitch 1 short straight stitch from across the middle of the crossed section.

DANISH KNOT

1. Start by bringing the needle up through the fabric at the top point of a triangle. Bring the needle back down through the fabric at the bottom right corner of the triangle, making a straight stitch.

2. Next, bring the needle up through the fabric in the bottom left corner of the triangle. Then slide the needle under the straight stitch with the tip pointed towards the bottom left corner. Gently pull the thread so that it wraps around the straight stitch.

3. Slide the needle under the straight stitch again, with the tip of the needle pointed towards the bottom left corner. This time, the tip of the needle should go over the thread coming out of the fabric. Again, gently tug the thread so that it is flush with the fabric.

4. To end the Danish knot, bring the needle back down through the fabric in the bottom left corner of the triangle.

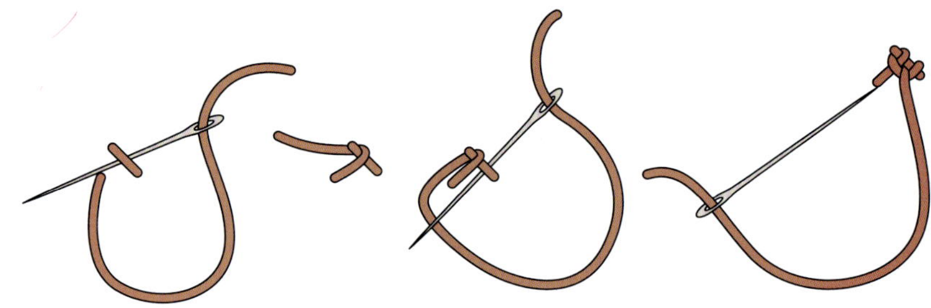

DETACHED CHAIN STITCH

See Lazy Daisy Stitch (page 23).

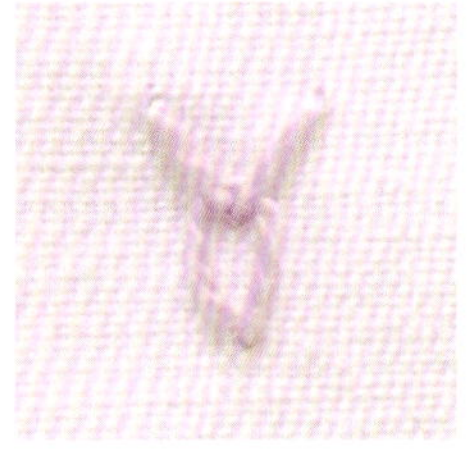

DETACHED WHEAT EAR STITCH

1. Work 2 straight stitches (page 35) from A to B and C to D.

2. Come up at E, pass the needle under the straight stitches, and go down at F.

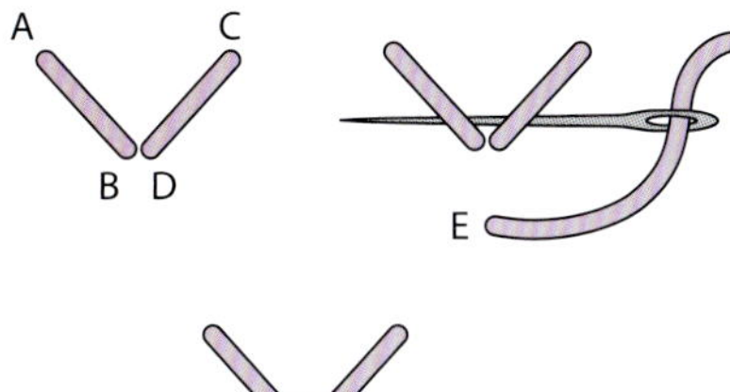

ERMINE STITCH

1. Work 1 straight stitch (page 35).

2. Work 2 straight stitches, crossing over the first from C to D and E to F.

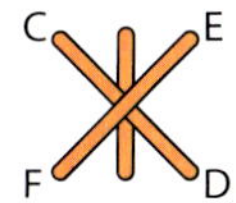

EYELET STITCH

1. Gentry pierce a hole in the fabric with an awl. Come up a A, then go down in to the center hole.

2. Come up again and work straight stitches around the center hole. Pull firmly to keep the hole open.

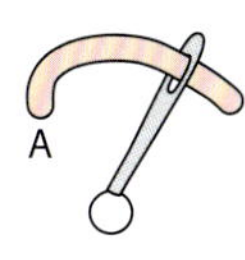

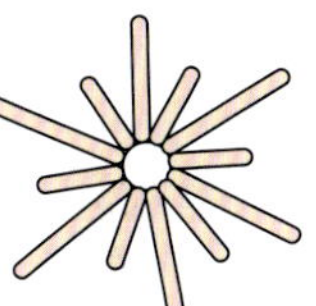

FAN STITCH

1. If you'd like, draw a square shape for your fan, with A on one corner. Come up at A and down at B, forming a straight stitch. Come up at C and down at A.

2. Take 5 more stitches, continuing to work around your square and coming down at A.

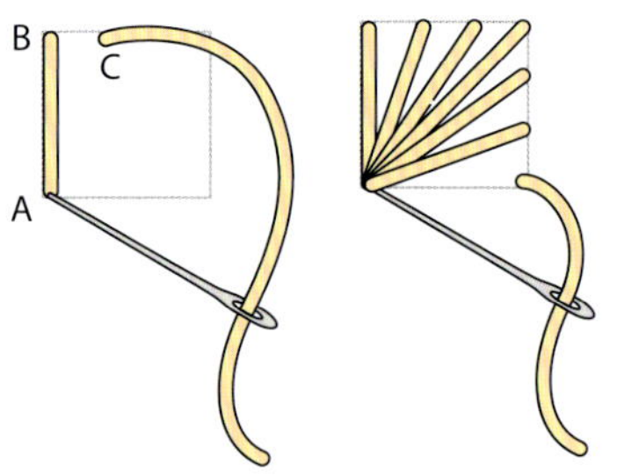

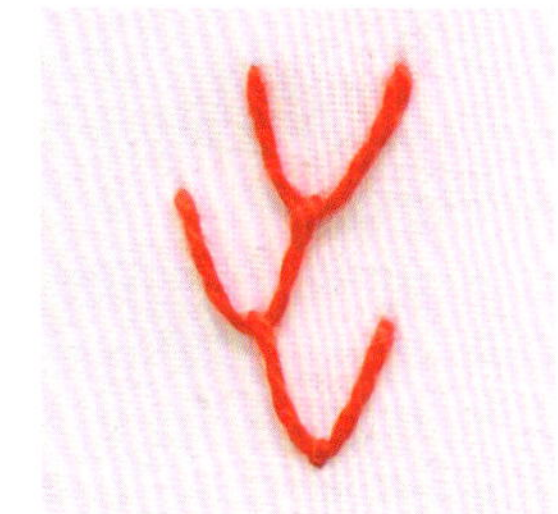

FEATHER STITCH

Work this stitch between 4 vertical lines.

1. Come up at A. *In one motion, go down at B and up at C. Wrap the working thread under the tip of the needle. Pull the needle through the fabric.

2. Repeat from *, working the next stitch below and in the opposite direction.

3. Repeat Steps 1 and 2 to finish the row. To end the stitch, go down at D.

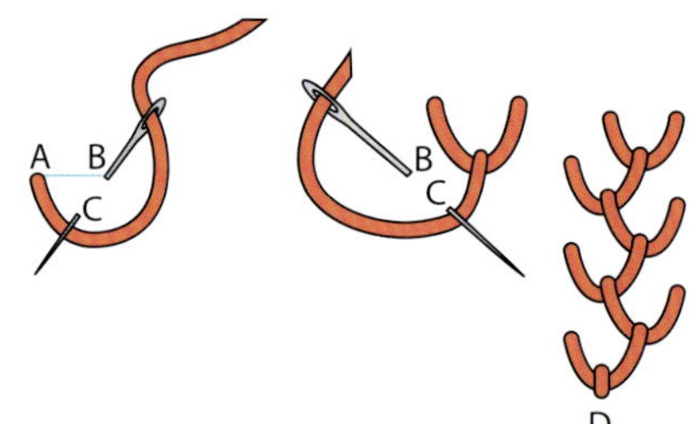

FEATHER STITCH SINGLE

Work this stitch between 2 vertical lines.

1. Come up at A. Follow Step 1 of the feather stitch (left) from *, with B directly across from A, and A and C on the line.

2. Repeat from * to finish the row. To end the stitch, go down at D.

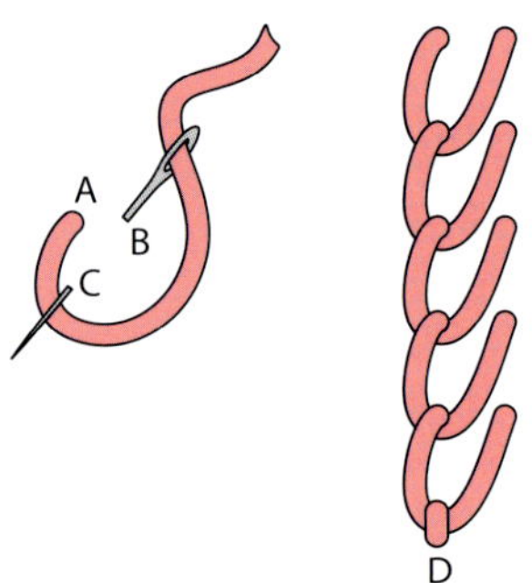

FERN STITCH MODERN

Draw a line or follow a seam.

1. Work a straight stitch (page 35) on the line. *Work 1 fly stitch with a long tail (right); the tail is the beginning of the next stitch, with D on the line. Note: A and B are even with the top of the straight stitch; C and D are the same length as the straight stitch.

2. Repeat from * to finish the row.

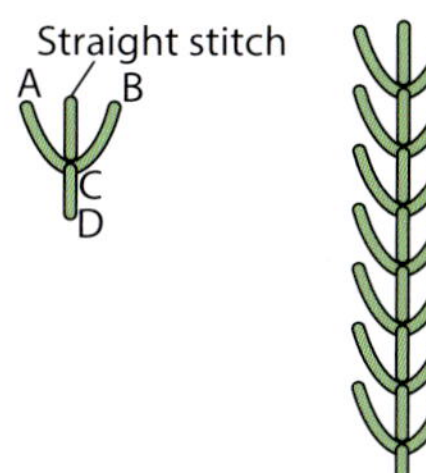

FISHBONE STITCH

1. Come up at A on the center line. Go down at B, then back up at C, keeping the thread on the right side of the needle (left side if left-handed).

2. Pull the thread through. With the thread on the left (on the right if you are left-handed), go down at D, then up at E.

3. Continue stitching to form the leaf.

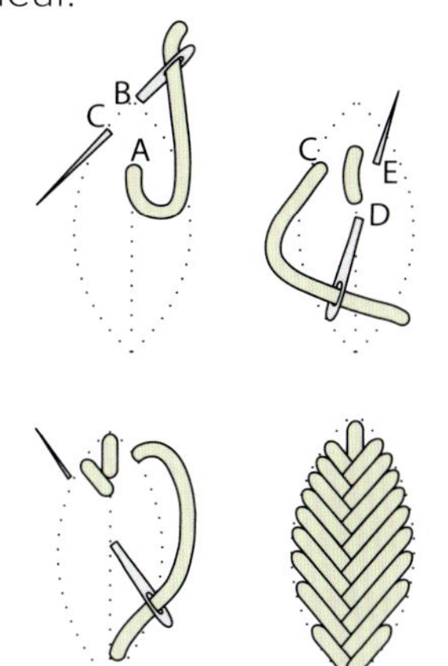

FLY STITCH

1. Come up at A. In one motion, go down at B and up at C. Wrap the working thread under the tip of the needle. Pull the needle through the fabric.

2. To end the stitch, go down at D or a short distance away for a long tail.

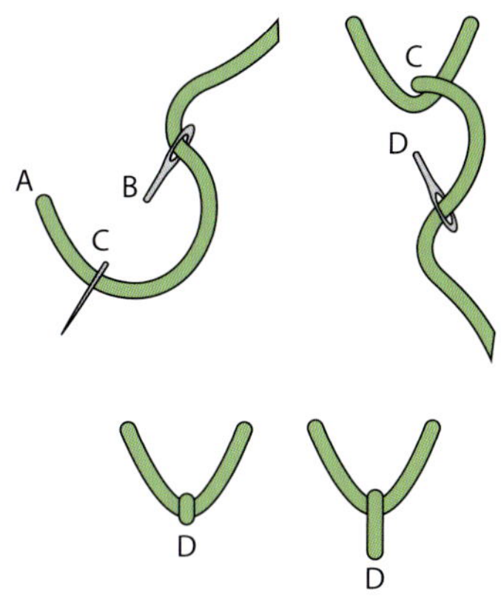

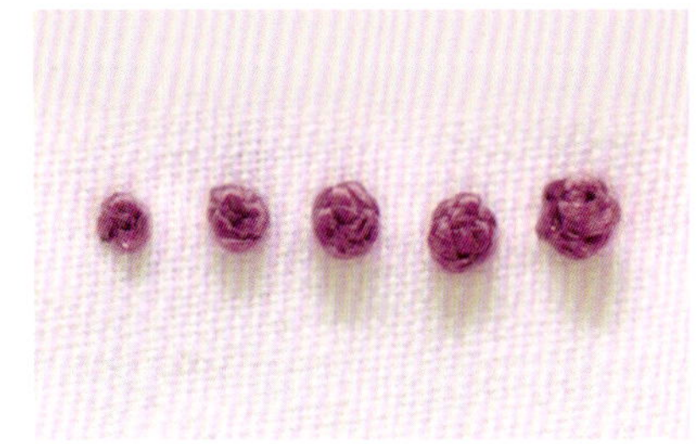

FLY STITCH STACKED

Work 1 fly stitch (page 19). Work the next 2 stitches below and around the previous stitch.

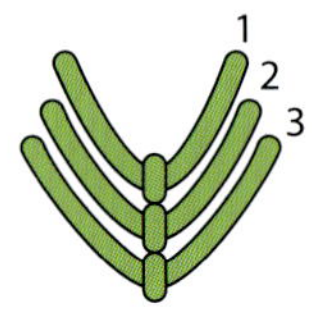

FRENCH KNOT STITCH

1. Come up at A. Holding the needle close to the fabric, wrap the thread around the needle 1–5 times.

2. Pull the thread tight; hold the end of the tail of thread with your thumb. Go down at B. Pull the needle and thread through the fabric.

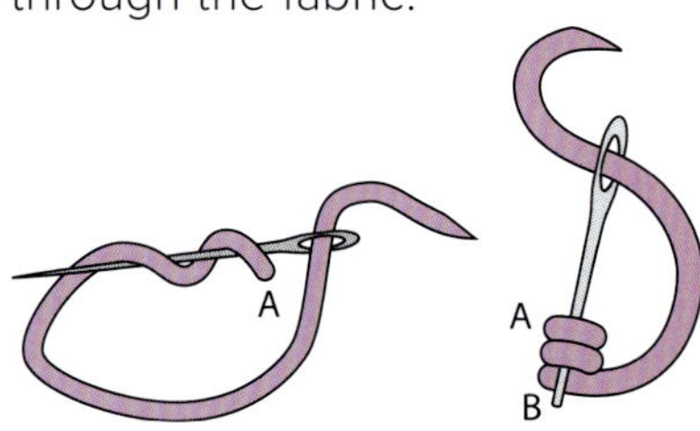

FRENCH KNOT STITCH FLOWER, 6 PETALS

1. Work a 3-wrap French Knot (left) for the center.

2. With the same thread or a different color, work 6 French knots, 2 wraps each, around the center in the order as shown, stitching close to the center or further away.

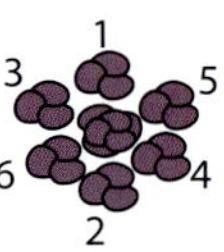

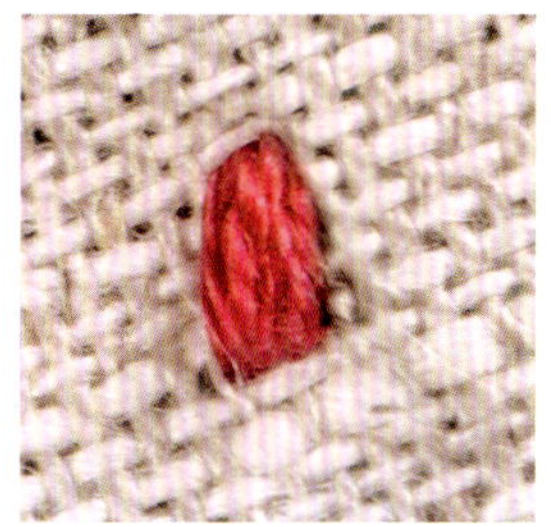

GRANITOS STITCH

1. Come up at A and go down at B.

2. Come back up at A in the same hole. Pull the thread through. Loop the thread to the left and go back down at B (through the same hole); pull through and position the thread on the left.

3. Come back up at A and loop the thread to the right. Go back down at B.

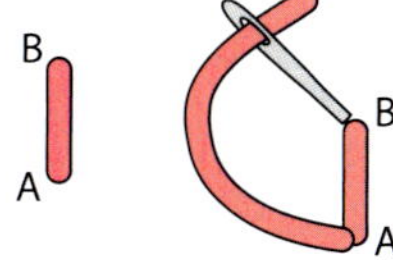

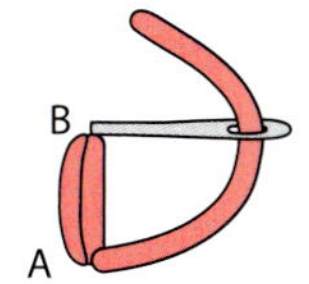

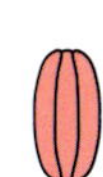

HEAVY CHAIN STITCH

This is also known as a braid stitch.

1. Come up at A, go down at B, then up at C. Slide the needle under the straight stitch between A and B, go down again at D as close to C as possible but not into it, and come up at E.

2. Slide the needle under the straight stitch again. Go down at F and up at G.

3. Slide the needle under the chain stitches and continue with the next stitch.

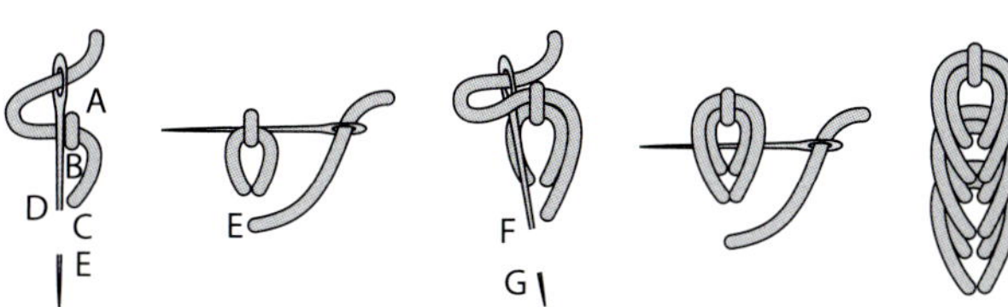

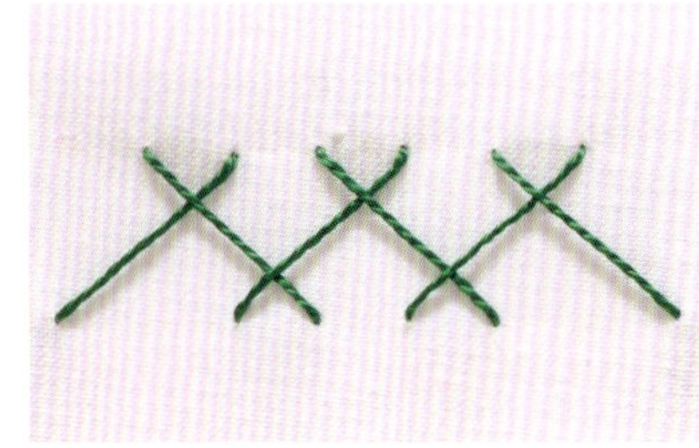

HERRINGBONE LADDER STITCH

This is a stitch that might be easier to understand the flow of the stitches in a video. Many are available online.

1. Stitch 2 rows of back stitches, offset by ½ a stitch.

2. Come up with a needle at the beginning of the first stitch of the bottom row. Pass the needle under the *2nd* stitch of the top row from bottom to top.

3. Pass the needle under the *1st* stitch of the top row from top to bottom and under the *3rd* stitch of the bottom row from the top to the bottom.

4. Pass the needle under the *2nd* stitch of the bottom row from bottom to top and under the *3rd* stitch on the top row from bottom to top.

5. Continue for the length of your ladder.

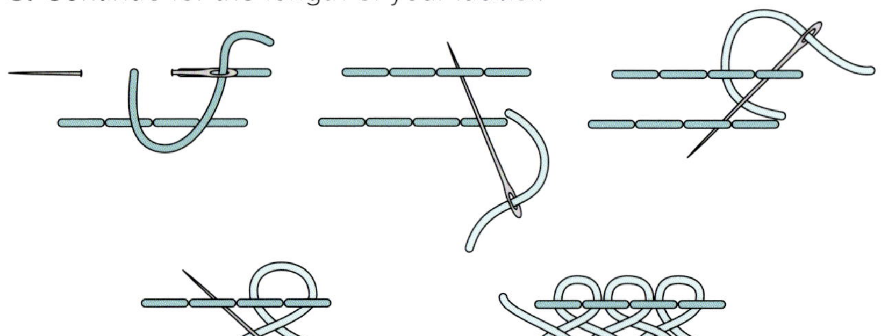

HERRINGBONE STITCH

Work this stitch between 2 horizontal rows.

1. Come up at A. *Backstitch the needle in one motion down at B and up at C. Pull the needle through the fabric. Repeat from *, going down at D and up at A.

2. Repeat Step 1 to finish the row. To end the stitch, go down at B or D.

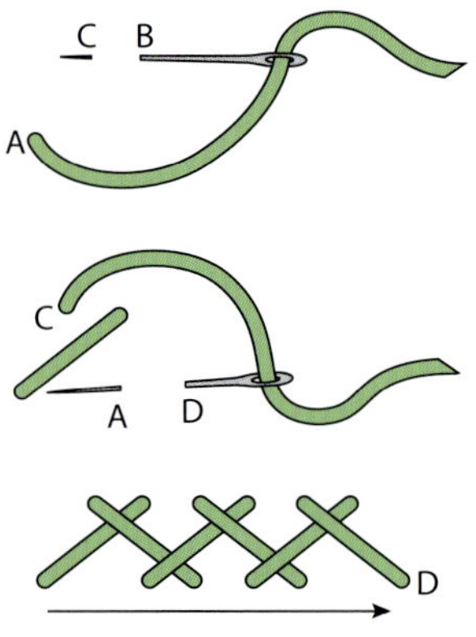

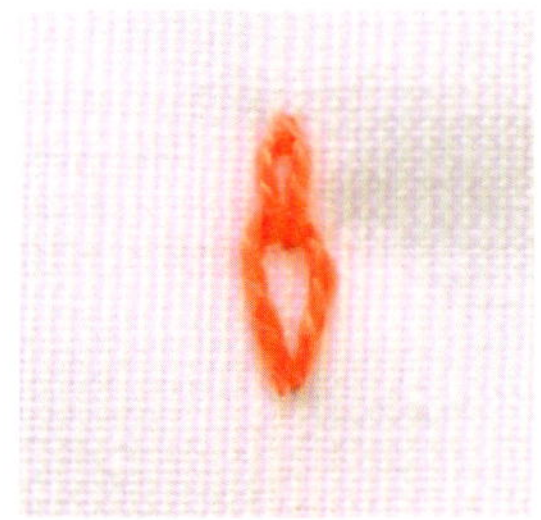

LAZY DAISY STITCH

1. Come up at A. In one motion, go down at B and up at C. Wrap the working thread under the tip of the needle. Pull the needle through the fabric.

2. To end the stitch, go down at D or a short distance away for a long arm stitch.

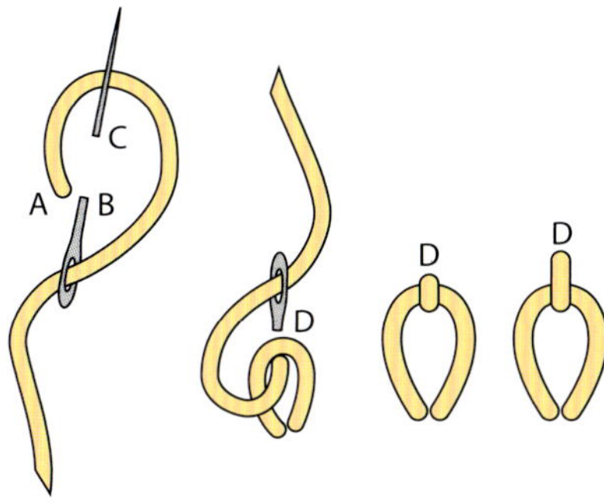

LAZY DAISY PIGGYBACK STITCH

Follow Step 1 of the lazy daisy stitch (left). Work a smaller stitch on the tip of and inside the first stitch. To end the stitch, go down at D.

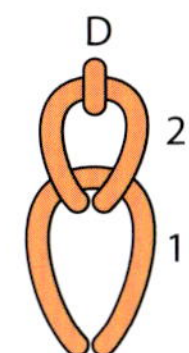

LAZY DAISY TULIP STITCH

Center: Work 1 lazy daisy stitch (left).

Sides: Come up at A. In one motion, go down at B and up at C; pull the needle through the fabric. To end the stitch, go down at D. Repeat for the other side.

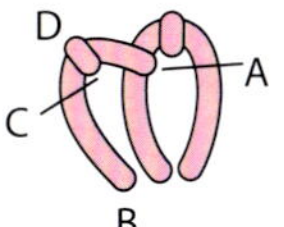

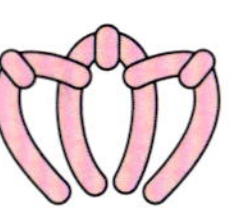

LAZY DAISY WITH FRENCH KNOT STITCH

1. Follow Step 1 of the lazy daisy stitch (page 23).

2. Holding the needle close to the fabric, wrap the thread 1–3 times around the needle. Go down at D. Pull the needle through the wrapped stitches and fabric.

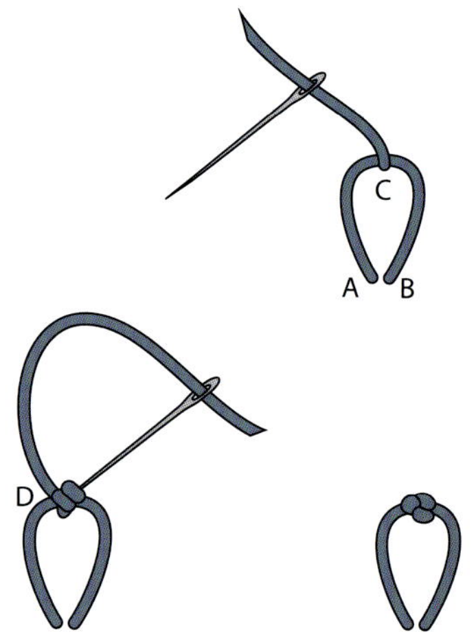

LEAF STITCH

Mark the shape to guide the stitches.

1. Come up at A, go down at B, and come up at C.

2. Work the stitches alternately on either center line to keep the spacing consistent. Continue in this manner, alternating from side to side, until the shape is filled.

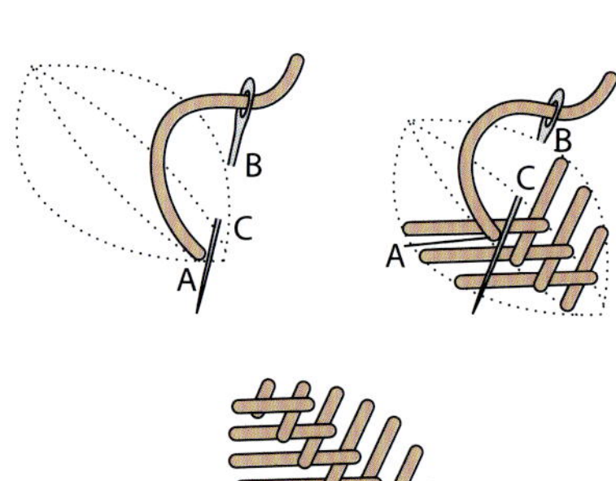

LONG & SHORT STITCH WITH SPLIT

The long and short stitch is great as a fill stitch for color changes. This twist on the stitch makes color changes more natural. See long and short stitch (page 25). Instead subsequent rows, going into the same hole as previous rows, you split the previous stitch, going into a random spot. Also, make your stitch lengths random.

LONG AND SHORT STITCH

1. Come up at A and go down at B, making a straight stitch the desired length; then come up at C.

2. Work the first row in alternating long and short satin stitches, keeping the outline of the shape even and defined.

3–4. Work the remaining satin stitch rows in equal lengths; vary the thread color to add shading. Use this stitch for shading or filling in large areas.

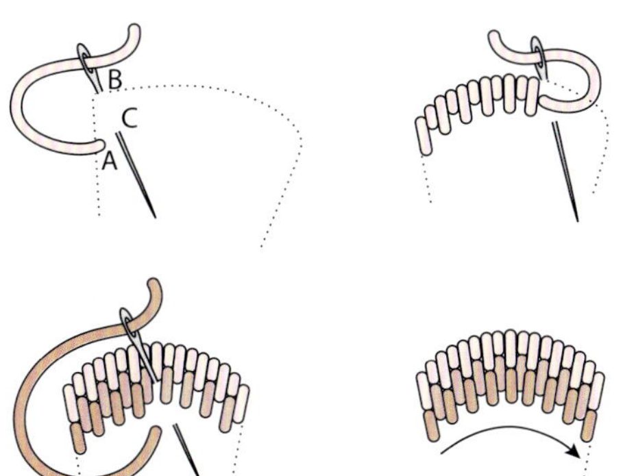

LOOPED TENDRIL STITCH

1. Follow Step 1 of the lazy daisy stitch (page 23). *In one motion, go down at B (outside of, and longer than the previous stitch) and up at C.

2. Repeat from *, stitching a third loop longer than the previous stitch. To end the stitch, go down at D.

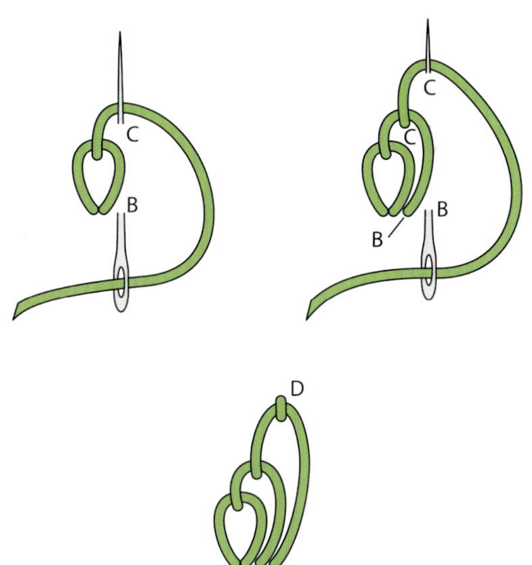

NEEDLE WEAVING BAR

Each bar is woven above the fabric with only the tip attached.

1. Come up at A. Form a loop and go down at B. Decide how wide the bar should be. Come up just below A at C.

2. Pass a paper clip through the loop to hold the loop off the fabric.

3. Weave over the bottom thread and under the top thread.

4. Come back over the top thread and under the bottom. After each pass, push the woven thread snugly down to the previous wraps.

5. After the loop is wrapped, remove the paper clip.

6–7. Make the bar curve by going into the fabric at D, just a bit shorter than the length of the bar.

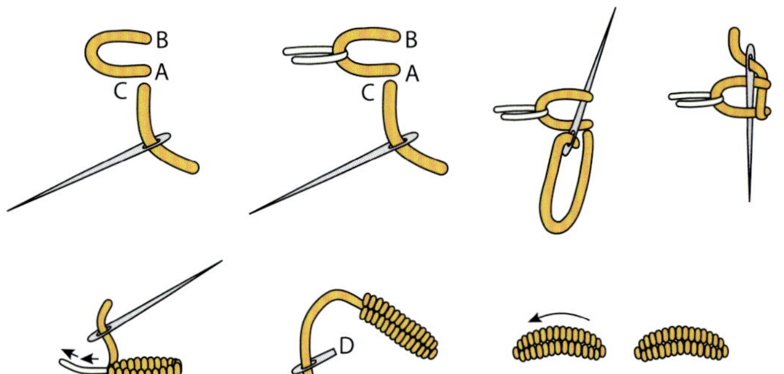

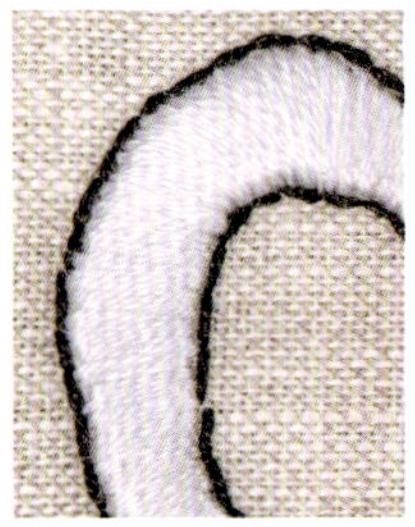

PADDED SATIN STITCH

1. Work 3–5 long straight stitches along your shape. These long threads will be the padding to be covered with satin stitches.

2. Follow instructions for satin stitches, page 30, and make a straight stitch across the foundation stitches at one end.

3. Continue to cover the padding evenly and thoroughly.

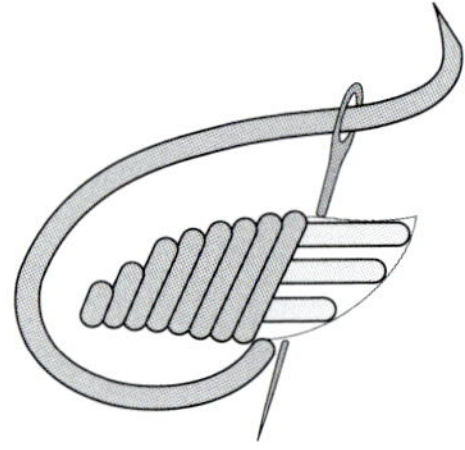

PALESTRINA KNOT STITCH

1. Come up at A. In one motion, go down at B and up at C.

2. *Wrap the thread over and under the stitch toward A. Wrap the thread a second time under the stitch toward B, wrapping the thread under the tip of the needle. Pull the thread gently around the stitch to form a knot.

3. In one motion, go down at D and up at E. A is now the end of the previous knot, D now becomes B, and E now becomes C.

4. Repeat from * to finish the row. To end the stitch, go down at D.

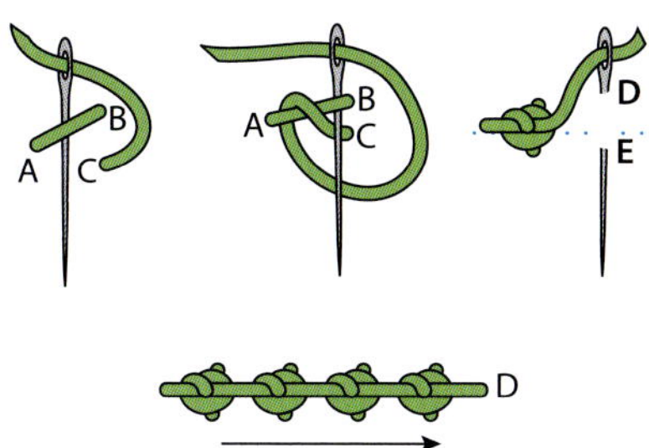

PEKING KNOT

1. Bring the needle out through at A. Make a loop of the thread a place it above the point A as shown in the illustration below.

2. Keeping the loop intact, put the needle in at B, inside the loop and extremely close to A, but do not pull the needle out yet.

3. Pull the thread to tighten the loop to the right size. Then pull the needle to tighten the knot.

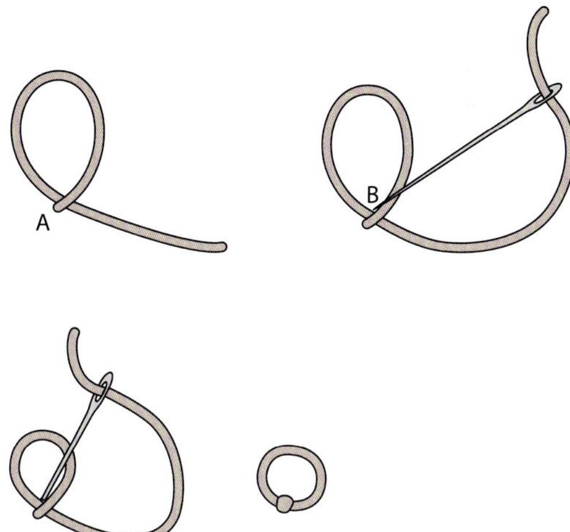

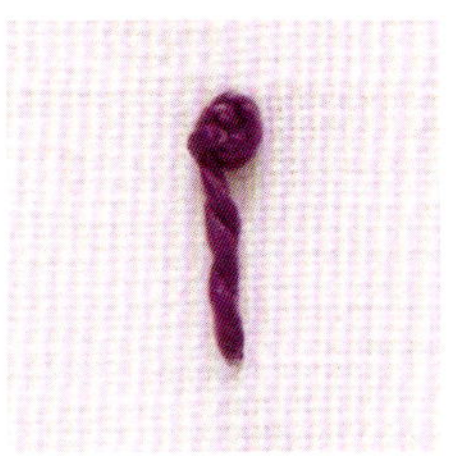

PISTIL STITCH

1. Come up at A. Holding the needle a short distance away and close to the fabric, wrap the thread 1–3 times over the needle.

2. Go down at B. Pull the thread tight around the needle and pull the needle through the fabric.

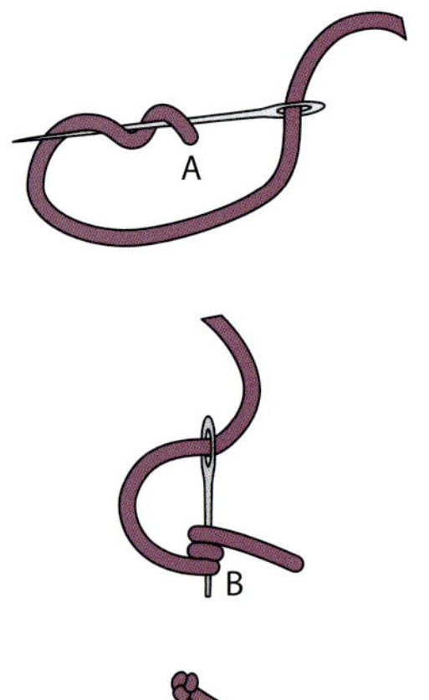

RAISED BUTTONHOLE STITCH

Note: *The raised buttonhole stitch is worked off the base of an embroidered stitch and does not go through the fabric, other than at the beginning and end of the stitch.*

1. Work 1 straight stitch (page 35) for the base.

2. Come up at A. *Pass the needle under the base stitch, and wrap the working thread under the tip of the needle. Pull the thread firmly around the base stitch.

3. Repeat from * to cover the base with stitches. To finish, go down at B.

Stitch courtesy of Melissa Galbraith (see Designers, page 122)

REVERSE CHAIN STITCH

1. Start by making a short back stitch at the beginning of the line.

2. Bring the needle up through the fabric a short distance away from the end of the back stitch at A.

3. Pass the needle underneath the back stitch. Gently tug the thread all the way through and bring the needle back down at B, making a small chain link.

4. Repeat adding chain links, sliding the needle underneath both strands of the previous chain link.

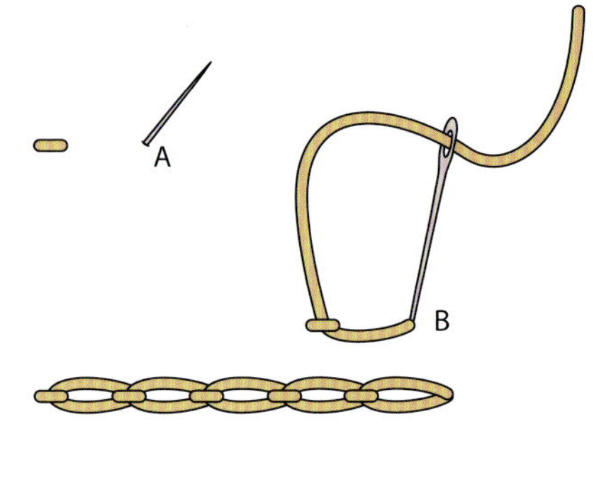

RHODES STITCH

The Rhodes stitch has a raised center because the series of straight stitches overlaps in the center.

1. Make straight stitch across the center of the desired shape.

2. Bring the needle up next to the start of the first stitch, stitch across the shape again, crossing the first stitch, and down on the other side of the first stitch.

3. Continue filling the shape, overlapping the stitches.

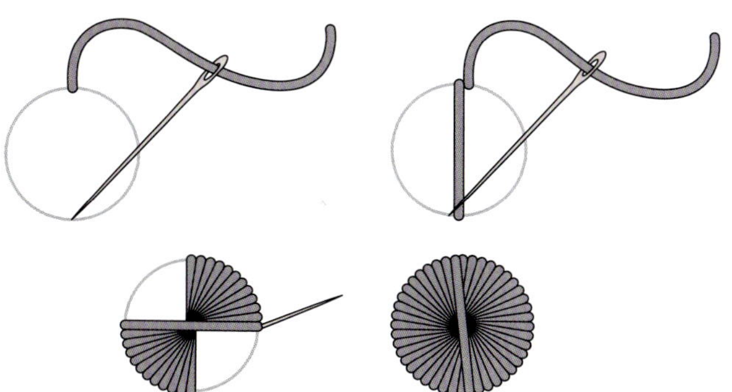

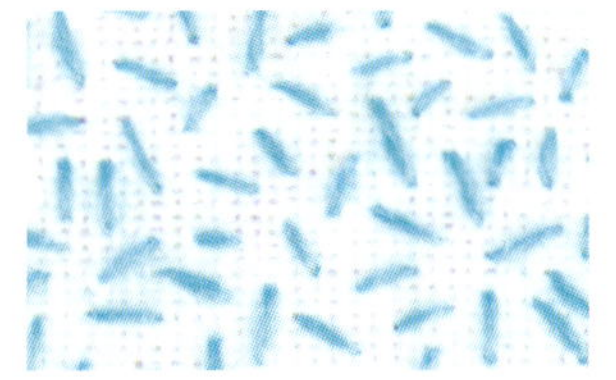

RICE STITCH

This stitch is sometimes referred to as scattered seed stitch.

1. Bring the thread out at A and make a small straight stitch, inserting the needle at B.

2. Bring the needle out a short distance away and make another stitch of the same length at a different angle. Continue in this way to fill the area, trying to make your stitches as randomly placed as possible.

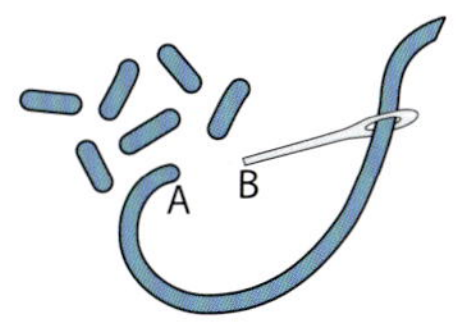

RUNNING STITCH

1. Come up at A. *In one motion, go down at B and up at C. Pull the needle through the fabric. C now becomes A.

2. Repeat from * to finish the row. To end the stitch, go down at B of the last stitch.

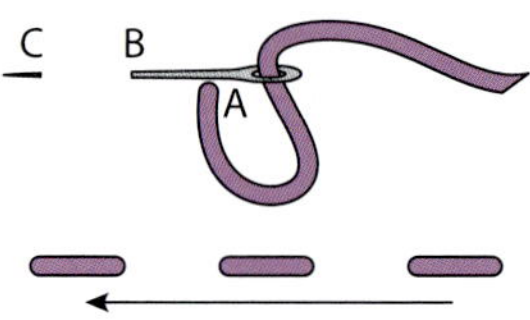

RUSSIAN CHAIN STITCH

Follow Step 1 of the lazy daisy stitch (page 23). Work a smaller lazy daisy stitch inside the first stitch to one side. Work another stitch on the other side.

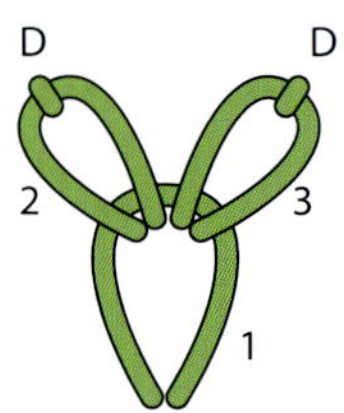

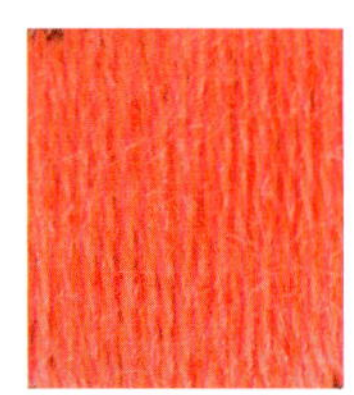

SATIN STITCH

1. Bring the needle up through the fabric and make a long stitch across the shortest side of the shape with the needle going down into the fabric on the other side of the shape.

2. Bring the needle back out right next to the first stitch and make a parallel stitch that lies as close as possible to your first. Continue working out to other end of the shape. You might find that it is easiest to start in the middle and work to one edge and then return to the middle and work to the other edge.

Satin stitches should be close together and parallel, with no gaps between them, to create a solid area of color.

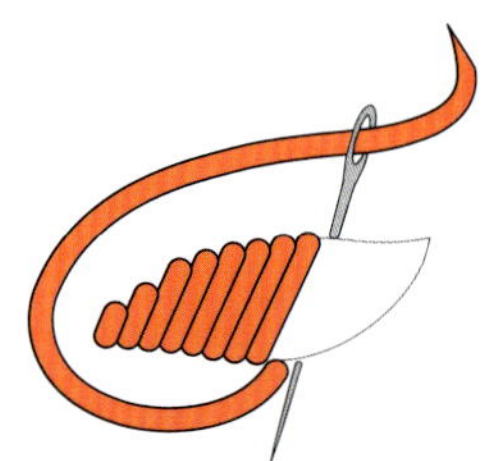

SCALLOPED BUTTONHOLE STITCH

This is stitch is also known as a chain stitch with raised button hole stitch.

1. Stitch 1 row of chain stitches (page 11).

2. With a different color of thread, come up next to the first stitch in the row. Follow Steps 2 and 3 of the raised buttonhole stitch (page 28), working over one side of the first stitch.

3. Repeat Step 2 to finish the row, alternating sides on the chain stitch row.

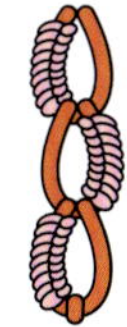

SCATTERED SEED STITCH

See Rice Stitch (page 29).

SEED STITCH

Stitch 1 straight stitch double (page 35) close together. Repeat, randomly filling in the section or space.

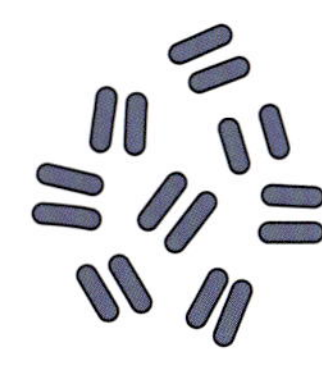

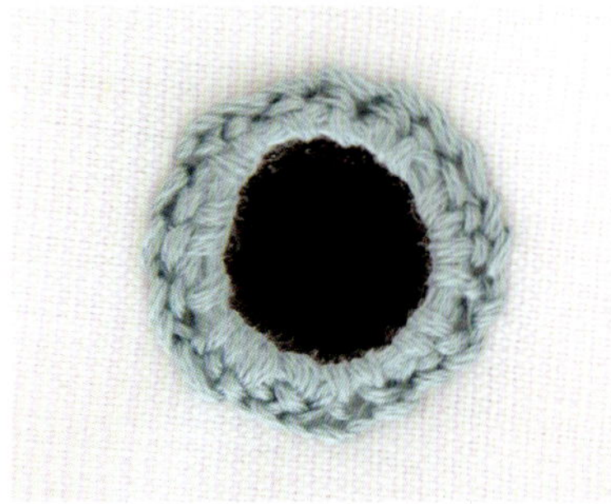

Stitch from Aimee Ray's *Doodle Stitching Embroidery Art*, C&T Publishing.

SHISHA EMBROIDERY

Shisha embroidery originated in ancient Persia and is traditionally used to attach tiny mirrors to clothing and wallhangings. It can also be used to attach any flat object, such as stones, shells, coins, bottle caps, sequins, or guitar picks.

1. To attach an object using the shisha stitch, hold it flat against the fabric and make 4 straight stitches across the object vertically and horizontally to hold it in place.

2. Next, stitch 4 more straight stitches across diagonally to form a star shape. Keep these stitches tight and not too close to the edge of the object.

3. Now bring the needle and floss up at A and under the straight stitches from the center at B. Pass the tip of the needle over the floss, making a tiny blanket stitch (page 8).

4. Repeat this step, then make another tiny stitch along the outside edge, catching the previous stitch and a tiny bit of fabric at C. Pass the needle over the floss again and pull it tight to the fabric.

5. Repeat this stitch all the way around the object.

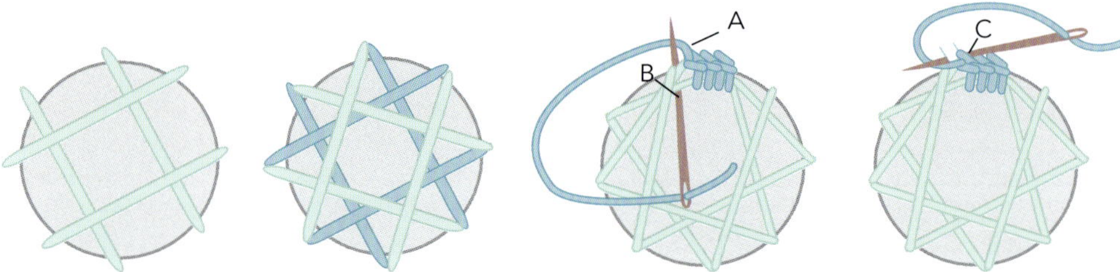

Stitch courtesy of Melissa Galbraith (see Designers, page 122)

SPIDERWEB ROSE STITCH

1. Draw a circle and then draw 5 equally spaced spokes. Work straight stitches (page 35) from the outer edge of the circle to center as shown. Knot and cut the thread.

2. Thread a chenille needle with 30″ (76.2cm) of your thread choice. Come up at A. Note: If you are working with 2 or more threads, twirl the needle to the right to twist the threads.

3. Weave the needle and thread over and under the spokes counterclockwise, pulling the thread through the spokes. To end the stitch, go down at B.

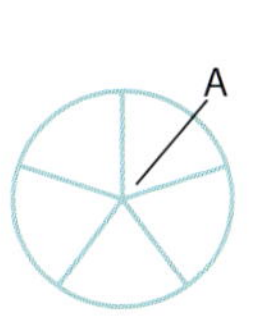

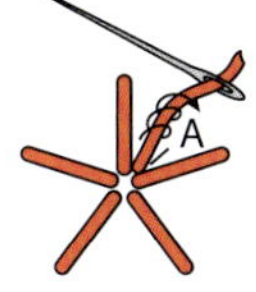

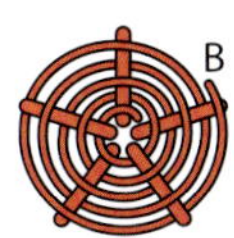

SPIRAL TRELLIS

The spiral trellis is a three-dimensional embroidery stitch that creates a raised dome on the front of the fabric.

1. Start by outlining the circle with the back stitch. These stitches should be short, because they're the anchors and base of the spiral trellis.

2. Next, bring the needle up parallel to the middle of the last back stitch made, on the inside of the circle.

3. From the inside of the circle, slide the needle underneath the back stitch. With the needle under the back stitch, slide the working thread around the needle counterclockwise. Then, continue pushing the needle out from underneath the back stitch. Gently tug so that the thread knot is flush with the back stitch and pulled towards the inside of the circle.

4. Repeat going all the way around the circle.

5. After the first row is stitched, add the second. These stitches are made by sliding the needle underneath the loop of thread between the thread knots in each row. Keep working around the circle until it is entirely filled in.

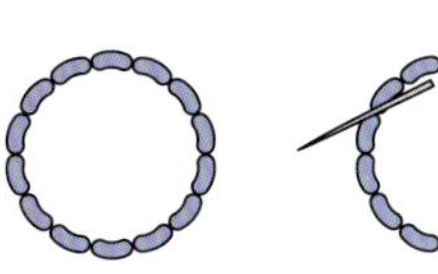

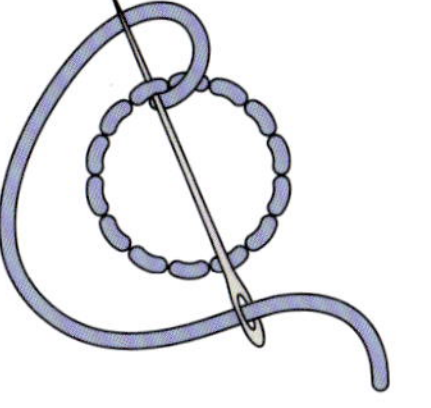

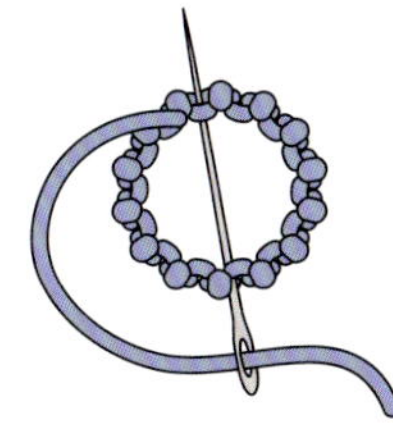

Continued on next page.

Continued from page 33.

6. To end this stitch, bring the needle down through the fabric in the middle of the circle.

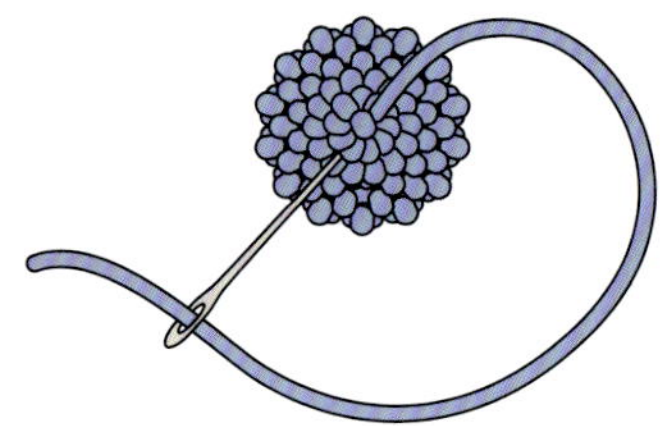

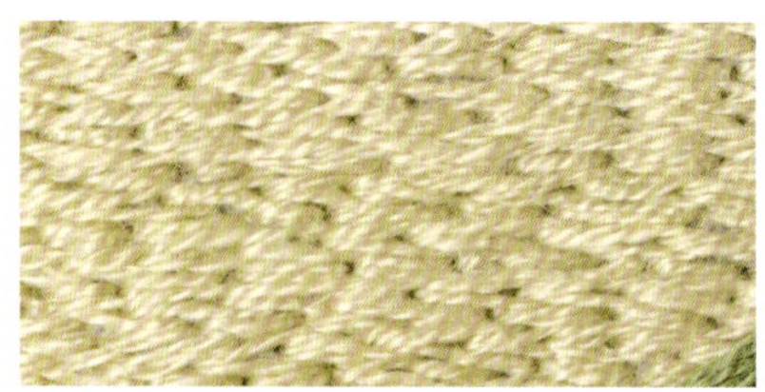

SPLIT BACK STITCH

This stitch is good for both outlining and for filling in spaces.

1. Come up at A, go down at B, and up at C.

2. Then bring the needle back down through the middle of the previous stitch at D, splitting the strands of the stitch apart.

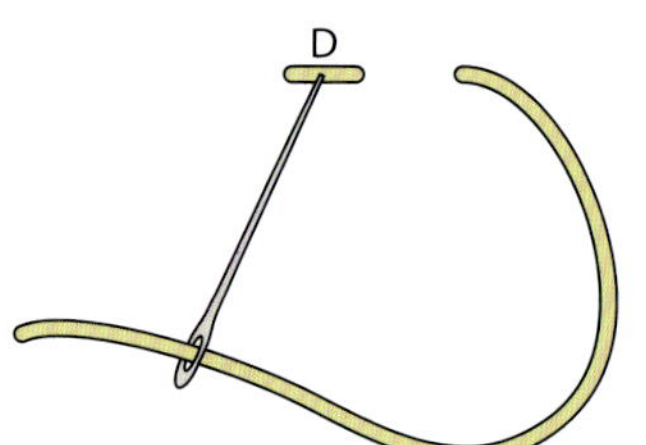

SPLIT STITCH

Thread the needle with a heavier thread such as size 3 or size 5 perle cotton.

1. Come up at A. *Backstitch the needle in one motion down at B and up at C piercing the working thread. Pull the needle through the fabric.

2. Repeat from * to finish the row. To end the stitch, go down at D.

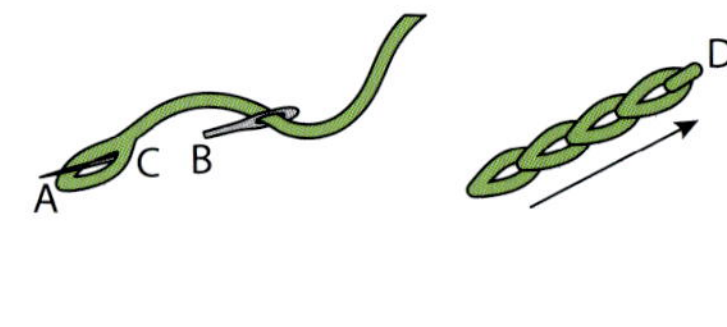

STAB STITCH

Stitch from Aimee Ray's *Doodle Stitching Embroidery Art*, C&T Publishing.

The stab stitch is a variation of the running stitch (page 30) using very tiny stitches. It's most often used to attach a piece of fabric to a background fabric. Use thread matching the fabric or one thread from a strand of floss. Bring the needle up at A and down at B, ⅛″ (3mm) from the edge of the fabric. Continue stitching all around the edge.

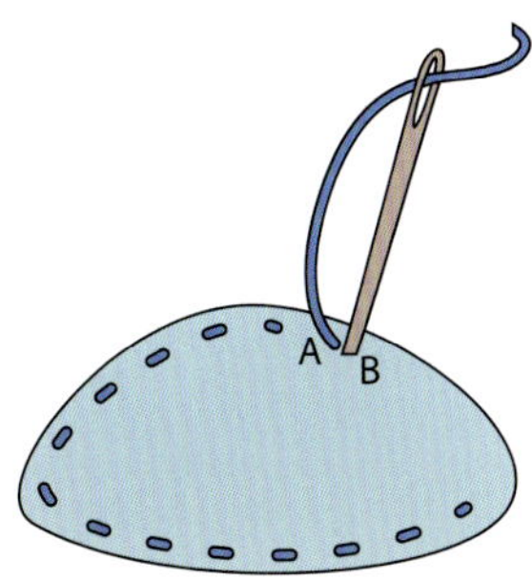

STAR EYELET STITCH

See Algerian Eye Stitch (page 7).

STEM STITCH

1. Come up at A, with the thread below the line. *Backstitch the needle in one motion down at B and up at C. Pull the needle through the fabric.

2. Repeat from * to finish the row, with C of the next stitch next to B of the previous stitch. To end the stitch, go down at B.

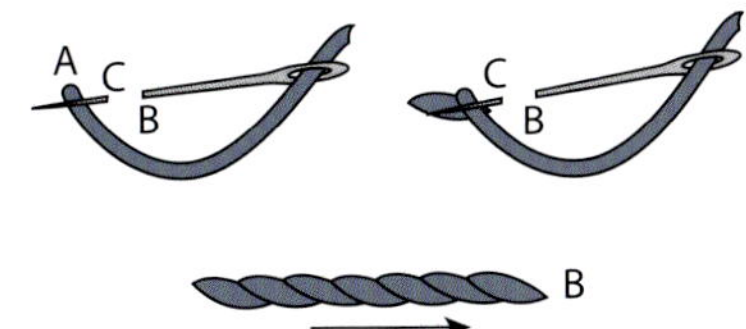

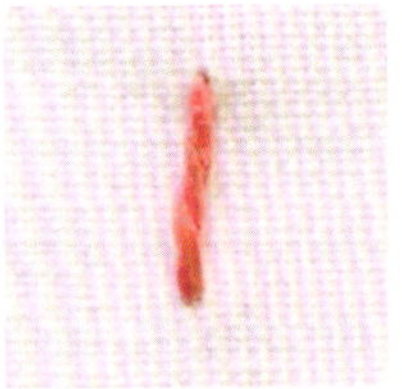

STRAIGHT STITCH

Come up at A and go down at B. This stitch can be worked vertically or horizontally.

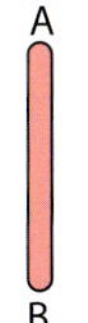

STRAIGHT STITCH DOUBLE

Work 2 straight stitches (at left) side by side in any direction.

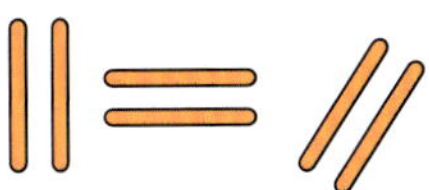

TRELLIS STITCH

1. Create parallel stitches in a horizontal or vertical direction across the fabric.

2. Then create lines that cross over the previous lines, forming a grid.

3. Add a tacking stitch using the same color thread or different. These should cross diagonally over where the horizontal and vertical lines meet. Bring the needle up just below the horizontal line and to the left of the vertical line, then bring the needle down across the horizontal line and to the right of the vertical line.

4. Repeat where all of the horizontal and vertical lines cross.

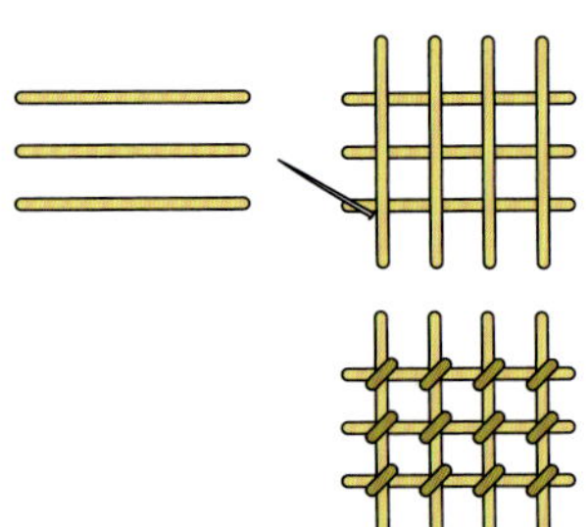

TURKEY RUG STITCH

This stitch is also called the turkey work stitch.

Work from the top of the fabric.

1. Go down at A and leave a ½″ tail. Holding the tail under your thumb, come up at B, and go down again at A.

2–3. Come up again at B and trim the second thread tail to match the first. To make a continuous row of uncut stitches, slide a pencil under each loop while stitching to keep the loops uniform.

Use for looped flowers; cut the loops to achieve a furry look.

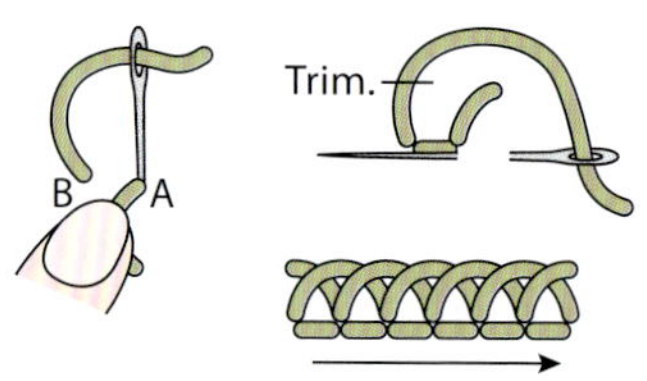

WEAVE STITCH

See Basket Weave Stitch (page 7).

WHIP STITCH

A whipstitch is a great way to close an opening in a 3-dimensional piece or to attach one element, such as a piece of felt, to another surface.

1. Bring your needle up from the back at A. Bring your needle down offset at B (the distance between A and B will be how long your stitch is), and back up again in C in the same motion. C should be parallel with A.

2. Continue in this way until the opening is closed or the pieces are joined, making sure that your stitches are even and equally spaced out.

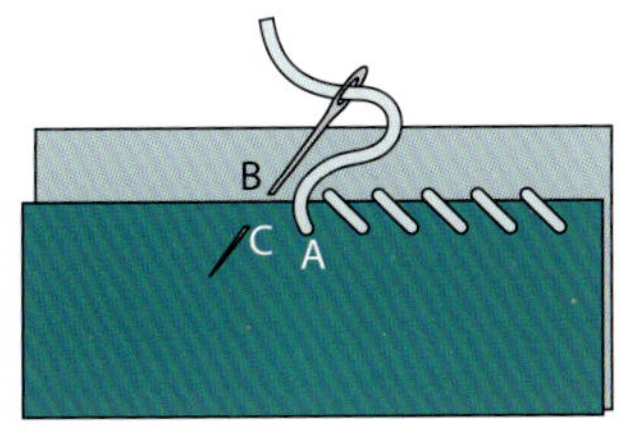

WOVEN SPIDER WEB STITCH

This stitch is also called the Whip-Stitch Rose.

1. Draw a circle with a smaller circle in the center. Work straight stitches (page 35) from the outer circle to the inner circle. Knot and cut the thread.

2. Come up at A. Note: If you are working with 2 or more threads, twirl the needle to the right to twist the threads.

3. Thread the needle over a spoke, and backstitch under the next 2 spokes. Gently pull the thread(s) to whip around the spoke.

4. Repeat Step 3, working around the spokes to the outer edges. To end, wrap the thread(s) over the previous spoke, and go down at B.

5. Fill the center with French knot stitches (optional).

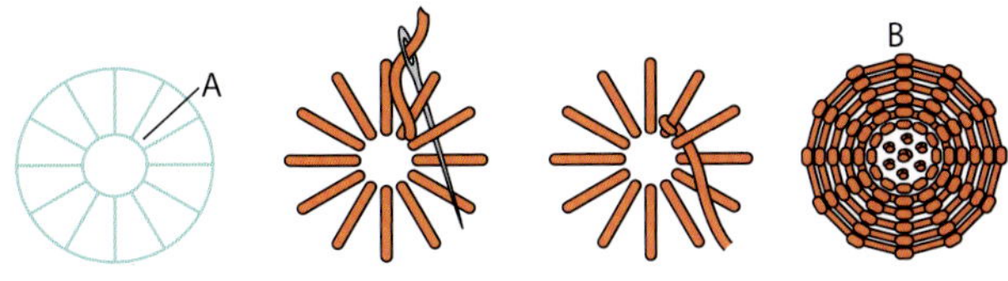

WOVEN WHEEL STITCH

See Spiderweb Rose Stitch (page 33).

SAMPLER PROJECTS

Tips for Stitching the Samplers

Each sampler follows the same format. First, review the required materials and threads. Then, keep the following tips in mind as you read the patterns and stitch each project:

- You only need 1 skein per thread color unless otherwise noted. Each color is assigned a letter.
- Refer to Stitches (page 6) for step-by-step tutorials of each stitch used in the projects. In each project, each stitch is assigned a number. Additionally, the stitch list notes how many strands of thread to use for each stitch. If the stitch requires a different number of strands in different areas of the embroidery, refer to the instructions.
- Embroider based on the number/letter (stitch/color) label in the stitch guide. The instructions are mostly supplementary, though they may provide useful clarification on more complex areas of the pattern.

Use the stitch guide as the pattern (following enlargement instructions as necessary). To access all the patterns as a downloadable PDF, scan the QR code or go to **tinyurl.com/11643-patterns-download**

BEACH WALK

By Megan Zaniewski

Finished Project:

10″ × 10″ (25.4 × 25.4cm)

Stitched Area: 7¼″ × 7¼″ (18.4 × 18.4cm)

This pattern is inspired by the time I spent living along the Gulf Coast, where my children and I would frequently take walks on the beach to look for seashells and play in the surf. The stitches I selected for this design create an ombre effect in both color and texture to mimic the way a wave transforms as it moves across the sand. I framed my final embroidery in a Modern Hoopla white-stained needlework frame.

MATERIALS

Tan cotton fabric: 11″ × 11″ (27.9 × 27.9cm) Kona cotton in Latte by Robert Kaufman Fabrics

Wooden embroidery hoop: 7½″ (190mm) Nurge No. 4

Frame for display (optional): Round 10″ (25.4cm)

Embroidery needles: Sizes 3 and 5

6-Stranded Embroidery Floss in the following colors:

A: Dark Turquoise (DMC 3808)

B: Turquoise (DMC 3809)

C: Light Turquoise (DMC 3810)

D: Aqua (DMC 598)

E: Pale Blue (DMC 747)

F: Light Grey (DMC #3756)

G: White (DMC BLANC)

H: Dark Orange (DMC 720)

I: Light Orange (DMC 3853)

J: Lavender (DMC 26)

K: Variegated Purple (DMC 4220)

STITCHES

1: Satin Stitch (3 strands)

2: Satin Stitch (6 strands)

3: Brick Stitch (6 strands)

4: Chain Stitch (6 strands)

5: Herringbone Ladder Stitch for the outline (3 strands)

6: Herringbone Ladder Stitch for weaving (3 strands)

7: Couch Stitch (laying thread, 6 strands)

8: Couch Stitch in contrast color (3 strands)

9: Peking Knot (3 strands)

10: French Knot (3 strands)

11: Woven Spider Web Stitch (6 strands)

12: Straight Stitch (6 strands)

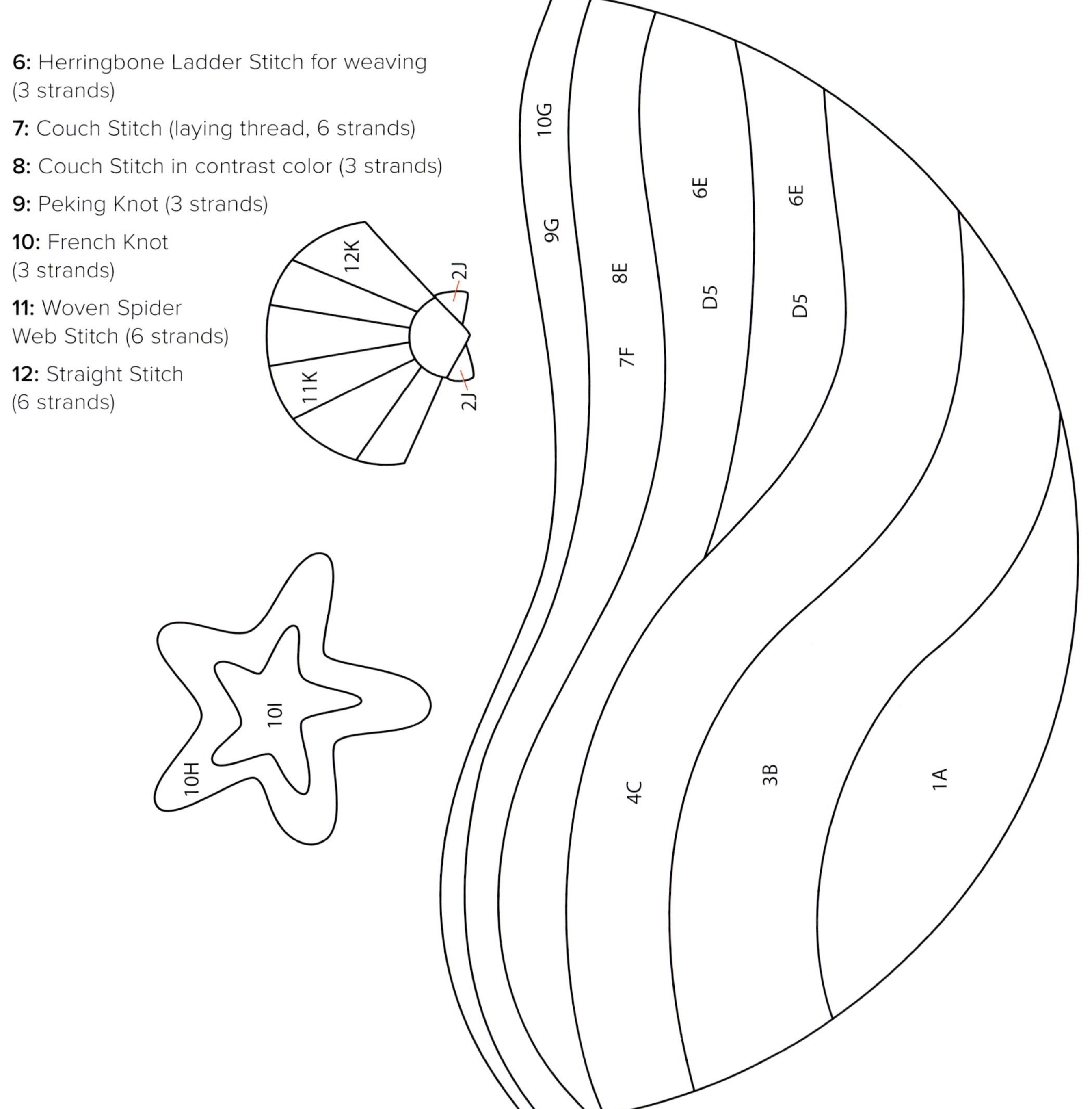

Instructions

PREPARATION

Trace the pattern onto a square of cotton fabric with carbon tracing paper or your preferred transfer method. Layer the pattern over the second piece of fabric and secure both in the embroidery hoop. *Note: I double my fabric so that it is completely opaque, and no stitching can show through from the backside.*

STITCHING

1. Begin at the bottom of the wave. Fill in the first 3 sections following the stitch guide.

2. For the next section, create the outline of the herringbone ladder stitch with 3 strands of aqua-colored thread. The woven part of the stitch should be completed with 3 strands of pale blue thread. Fill in the two rows of herringbone ladder stitch. The rows may overlap slightly.

3. Couch stitch 6 strands of the light grey thread with contrasting pale blue thread. Continue couching the thread in rows until the section is filled.

4. Fill the sea foam layer following the stitch guide. Vary the size of each knot to create more variety and dimension.

5. Embroider the scallop shell with a woven spider web stitch. Work the woven stitches from right to left. When you reach the end of a row, bring the needle down and pass under the backside of the fabric to begin the next row from the right side again. Continue until the shell's ridges are covered. Add straight stitches along the outside of the shell to fill out the shape as needed.

6. Embroider the starfish using the stitch guide.

Finishing

I opted to display this piece in a round 10″ (25.4cm) Modern Hoopla needlework frame. The embroidery hoop fits snugly inside the frame so there is no need to take any extra steps to finish it.

WILDFLOWER WINDMILL

By Louise Watson

Finished project: 5″ × 5″ (12.7 × 12.7cm)

Stitched area: 4¾″ × 4¾″ (12.1 × 12.1cm)

I am always inspired by flowers and buildings. Having always fancied stitching a windmill, I thought of the title *Wildflower Windmill* and developed the scene from there. The colours are fresh and spring-like, and the variations of stitches make it a good tool to practice or to take your time on a textured project that produces a lovely calming scene.

MATERIALS

Medium-weight natural calico cotton: 7″ × 7″ square

Wooden embroidery hoop: 5″ (12.7cm)

Embroidery needle: Size 3

6-Stranded Embroidery Floss in the following colors:

A: Light Brown (DMC 840)

B: Salmon Pink (DMC 3712)

C: Clay Pink (DMC 3778)

D: White (DMC BLANC)

E: Pale Pink (DMC 23)

F: Golden Yellow (DMC 972)

G: Bright Green (DMC 907)

H: Green (DMC 470)

I: Bright Pink (DMC 602)

J: Blush Pink (DMC 3354)

K: Yellow (DMC 444)

L: Cornflower Blue (DMC 3838)

M: Brown (DMC 838)

N: Lilac (DMC 153)

O: Red (DMC 347)

STITCHES

1: Basket stitch (6 strands)

2: Satin stitch (3 strands)

3: Brick stitch (6 strands)

4: Back stitch (3 strands)

5: French Knot

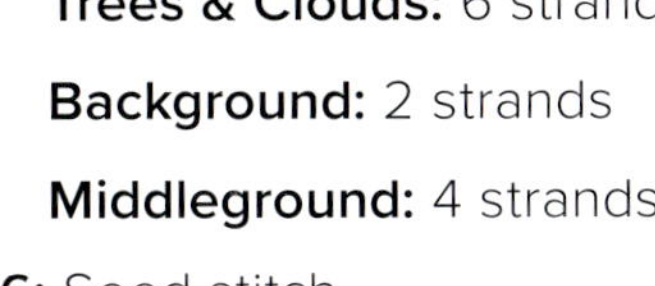

Trees & Clouds: 6 strands

Background: 2 strands

Middleground: 4 strands

6: Seed stitch

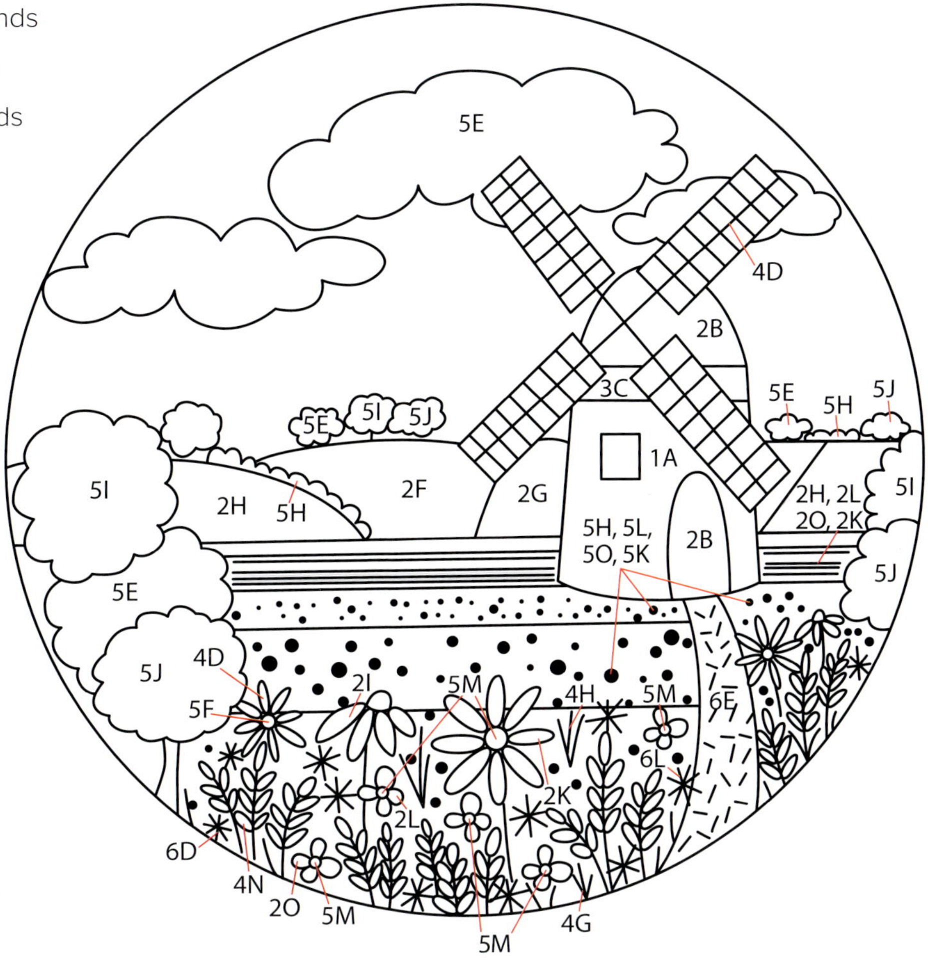

5E
4D
2B
3C
5E 5H 5J
5E 5I 5J
1A
5I 2H 5H 2F 2G
2H, 2L
2O, 2K
5I
5H, 5L,
5O, 5K
2B
5J
5E
5J 4D
2I 5M 4H 5M
5F 6E
6L
2K
2L
6D
4N
2O 5M
5M
4G

Instructions

PREPARATION

Trace the Wildflower Windmill pattern onto the fabric. Insert the fabric into the 5″ × 5″ hoop.

STITCHING

1. Using 6 strands of light brown, stitch 7 vertical lines on the windmill. Then, fill that section with Basket stitch. Fill the door and the top with satin stitch in 3 strands of salmon pink.

2. Satin stitch the middle section of the windmill with brick stitch in 6 strands of clay pink. Use long perpendicular backstitches to stitch the sails of the windmill with 2 strands of white. Seed stitch the path in pale pink.

3. Satin stitch the hills and trees following the stitch guide. Use single long satin stitches at the base of the hills. Fill the clouds with French knots in pale pink.

4. Stitch the flowers following the stitch guide. Pack the French knots densely and evenly distribute the colors to fill the area between the hills and the foreground flowers.

5. Fill the space between the flowers in the front and mid sections with 3 strands of green and bright green vertical backstitches.

FINISHING

Trim around the excess fabric around the hoop and back it in this hoop, or move it to one of your choice.

SPOOL DANCER

By Laura Wasilowski

Finished Size: 8″ × 11″ (20 × 28cm)

Stitched Area: 7½″ × 10½″ (19 × 27cm)

Spool Dancer is inspired by my love of hand embroidery that is colorful, whimsical, and densely stitched. Not a day passes that I don't have a needle and thread in my hand and a sense of joy when stitching. Embroidery is a wonderful art form full of texture, pattern, and color that warms the heart. Unlike most embroidery projects, this sample requires no hoop! Unless otherwise noted, the thread colors were hand-dyed for this project.

MATERIALS

Light green medium-weight wool: 8″ × 11″ (20 × 28cm) for the background

Blue felt: 9″ × 12″ (23 × 31cm) for backing the hoop

Embroidery needles: Sizes 3 and 5

Scissors

Tracing paper

Contrast color sewing thread for transferring the pattern

Black fine-point marker

Straight pins

Wool pressing mat

Steam iron

Rotary cutter and mat

Size 8 Perle Cotton in the following colors:

A: Turquoise

B: Variegated Red/Orange

C: Variegated Green

D: Rust

E: Medium Green

F: Dark Green

G: Red

Size 12 Perle Cotton in the following colors:

I: Orange

J: Black (DMC 310)

K: Gray

L: White (DMC BLANC)

STITCHES

1: Running stitch

2: Stem stitch

3: Chain stitch

4: French knot

5: Lazy daisy

6: Straight stitch

7: Scattered seed stitch

8: Blanket stitch

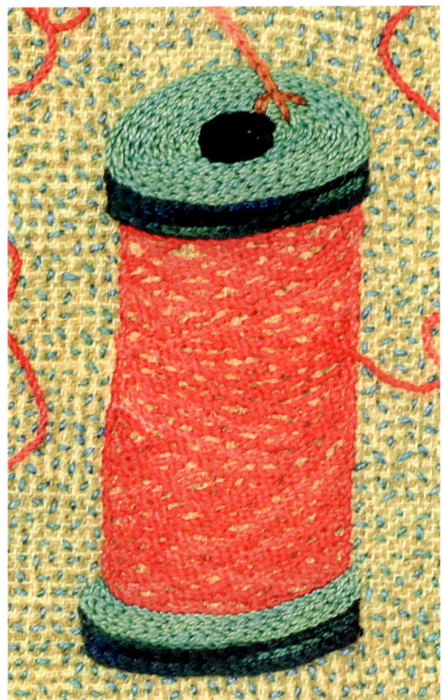

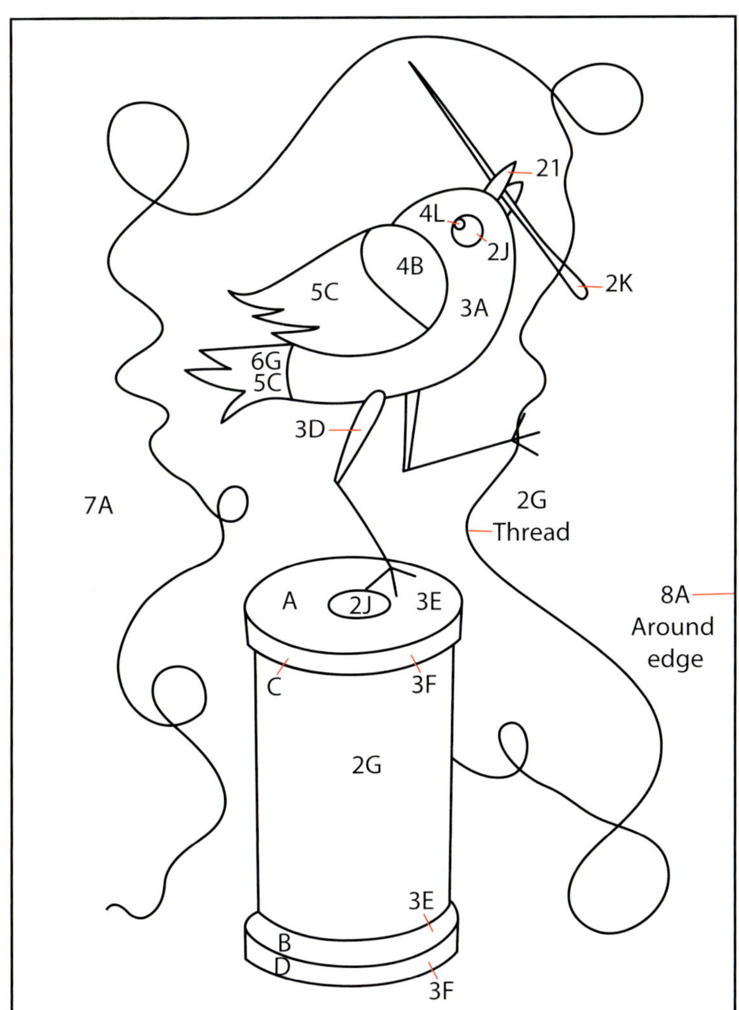

Enlarge 200% to use as template.

Instructions

TRANSFER THE PATTERN

1. Place tracing paper on the pattern, and trace it with the black marker.

2. Center the tracing paper on the wool fabric. Pin it into place.

3. Stitch the paper to the fabric following the black marker lines with a running stitch. Use the contrast sewing thread.

4. After stitching the pattern outline, remove the paper. Use the tip of a pin to score the paper and gently rip it away. The running stitches define the edges of the design and will be removed after embroidering the project.

STITCH THE BIRD

1. Use stem stitches to outline the bird's body and wing with turquoise thread.

2. Use stem stitches to outline the beak with orange thread. Fill in the beak with parallel rows of stem stitches.

3. Use stem stitches to outline the eye with black thread. Fill in the eye with stem stitches.

4. Use a French knot to stitch a dot on the eye with white thread.

5. Use French knots to fill the wing cap using red/orange thread.

6. Use lazy daisy stitches to fill in the wing tips and tail with variegated green thread.

7. Use straight stitches to fill in the loops of the lazy daisy stitches on the tail with red thread.

8. Use rows of chain stitches to fill in the body with turquoise thread, spiraling the rows around the eye.

9. Use 2 rows of chain stitches to make the top of the legs. Use 1 row of chain stitches to make the lower legs and feet with rust thread.

10. Remove the running stitches that marked the fabric for the bird shape.

STITCH THE NEEDLE AND SPOOL

1. Use stem stitches to outline the needle with gray thread. Stitch the outline under the top of the bird's beak and over the bottom of the beak with the same color. Fill in the needle shape with stem stitches, leaving a small opening for the needle eye.

2. Use stem stitches to outline the oval on the spool top (area A) with black thread.

3. Use stem stitches to fill in the oval with black thread.

4. Use stem stitches to outline areas A and B of the spool with medium green thread.

5. Use chain stitches to fill in the A and B areas with medium green thread.

6. Use stem stitches to outline areas C and D of the spool with dark green thread.

7. Use chain stitches to fill in the C and D areas with dark green thread.

8. Use stem stitches to outline the thread spool center with red thread.

9. Use stem stitches to make the thread lines crossing from side to side on the spool with red thread.

10. Use stem stitches to make the loose piece of string with red thread. Stitch the line from the right side of the spool, through the bird's foot and eye of the needle, and around the bird.

11. Remove the running stitches that marked the fabric for the needle and spool shapes.

BACKING AND BACKGROUND

1. Place the design face down on a wool pressing mat, and use a steam iron to flatten the fabric. Trim the design square if necessary.

2. Pin the design to the backing fabric. Stitch ½″ (1.2cm) running stitches around the edge of the piece to secure it to the backing fabric.

3. Blanket stitch around the edge of the main fabric, attaching it to the backing fabric with turquoise thread.

4. Remove the running stitches that held the design in place.

5. Use scattered seed stitches to densely fill in the background fabric with turquoise thread.

6. Trim the backing fabric to ¼″ (6mm) larger than the main fabric of the edge of the design.

TINY TERRARIUM

By Aimee Ray

Finished Project: 6″ × 6″ (15.2 × 15.2cm)

Stitched Area: 3¼″ × 3″ (8.3 × 7.6cm)

Terrariums are so magical: tiny, secret worlds that live on your shelf! What better way to bring life and color into your world. This elegant little glass globe houses succulents, leafy vines and tiny mushrooms. What else might be hiding beneath them? Create a special space for yourself as you stitch up these pretty little plants.

MATERIALS

White cotton fabric: 8″ × 8″ (20.3 × 20.4cm)

Embroidery hoop: 6″ (15.2cm)

Embroidery needle: Size 3 or size 5

6-Stranded Embroidery Floss in the following colors:

A: Light Green (DMC 3348)

B: Green (DMC 470)

C: Aqua (DMC 3817)

D: Turquoise (DMC 3816)

E: Dark Turquoise (DMC 3848)

F: Pink (DMC 758)

G: Dark Pink (DMC 3778)

H: Grey (DMC 3023)

I: Brown (DMC 3032

J: Cream (DMC 3866)

STITCHES

1: Stem stitch

2: Straight stitch

3: Satin stitch

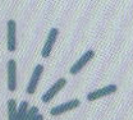

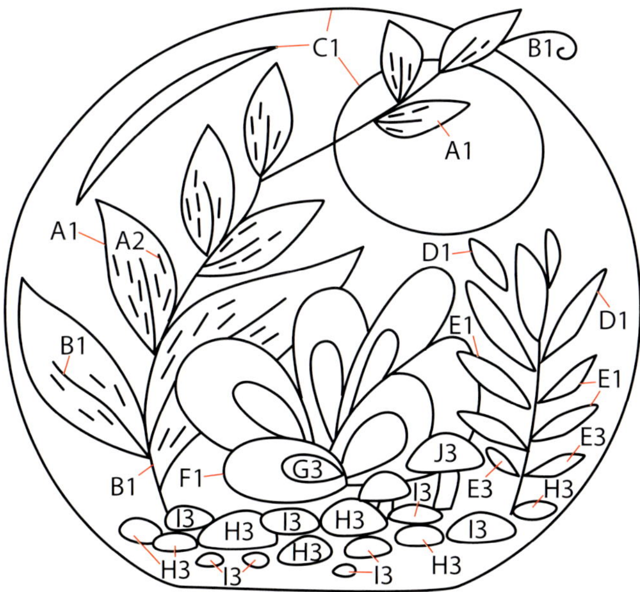

Instructions

PREPARATION

1. Trace the pattern onto the cotton fabric using your preferred method.

2. Stretch the fabric in the embroidery hoop.

STITCHING

1. Outline the terrarium globe with 3 strands of stem stitch in Aqua.

2. Stitch the left green leaf stem, outline, and details with stem stitches and straight stitches following the stitch guide (2 strands).

3. Stitch the central pink succulent with stem stitches and satin stitches following the stitch guide (2 strands).

4. Stitch the right blue leaves and stem with stem stitches and satin stitches following the stitch guide (2 strands).

5. Stitch the foreground mushrooms and rocks with satin stitches following the stitch guide (2 strands).

HARVEST MOON

By Aimee Ray

Finished Project: 6″ × 6″ (15.2 × 15.2cm)

Stitched Area: 4½″ × 4″ (11.4 × 10.2cm)

Step out into a crisp Autumn night, and look up at the full, buttery moon. The chilly air, rich scent of fallen leaves, and fat, ripe pumpkins will tickle your nose! Come stargaze and dance with wild foxes, then cozy in with a warm drink and a blanket and embroider this whimsical celebration of your favorite season.

MATERIALS

White cotton fabric: 8″ × 8″ (20.3 × 20.4cm)

Embroidery hoop: 6″ (15.2cm)

Embroidery needle: Size 3 or size 5

6-Stranded Embroidery Floss in the following colors:

A: Yellow (DMC 3822)

B: Gold (DMC 3852)

C: Orange (DMC 3853)

D: Light Orange (DMC 402)

E: Dark Pink (DMC 352)

F: Pink (DMC 353)

G: Brown (DMC 435)

H: Dark Brown (DMC 433)

I: Cream (DMC Ecru)

STITCHES (2 STRANDS)

1: Stem Stitch

2: Straight Stitch

3: Back Stitch

4: Satin Stitch

5: Lazy Daisy

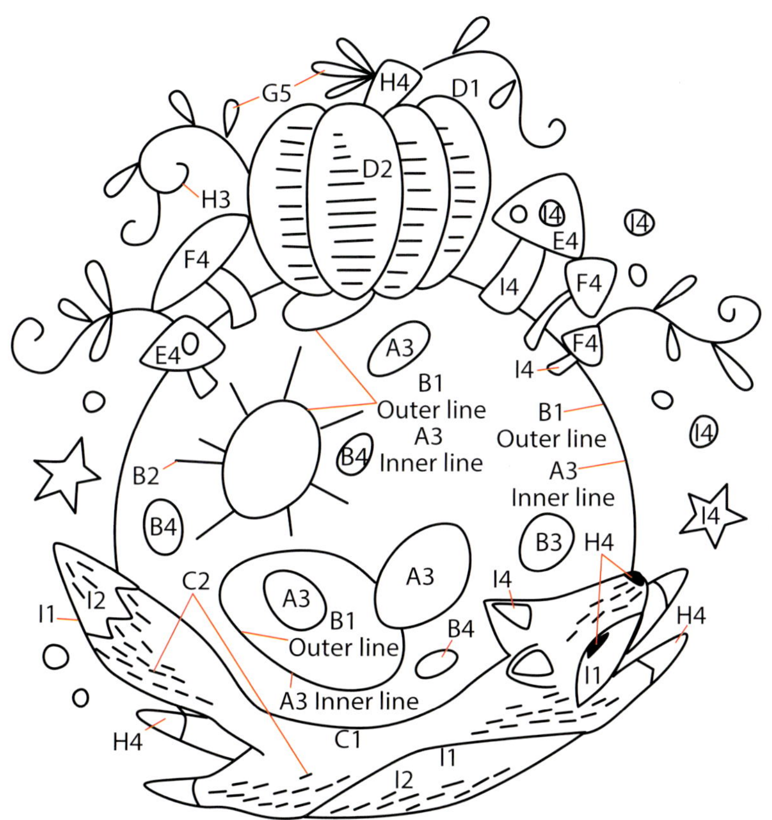

Instructions

1. Trace the pattern onto the cotton fabric using your preferred method.

2. Stretch the fabric in the embroidery hoop.

3. Stitch the fox using straight stitches, stem stitches, and satin stitches by following the stitch guide. Outline the body, then fill in the details.

4. Embroider the moon following the stitch guide. Stitch all the way up to the top of the moon where the pumpkin will sit. Stitch the dots and stars outside of the moon.

5. Stitch the mushrooms and pumpkin at the top of the moon following the stitch guide. Satin stitch over the moon outline with the mushroom stems. Use lazy daisy stitches for the leaves.

GARDEN CAT

By Aimee Ray

Finished Project: 6″ × 6″ (15.2 × 15.2cm)

Stitched Area: 3″ × 3¾″ (7.6 × 9.5cm)

If you're lucky enough to make friends with the elusive faery Garden Cat, she will use her green paw to help your flowers grow. But, watch out! She's just as favorable to wild weeds! Grow your own tiny garden in stitches with this colorful kitty—no green thumb required. It's a purrfect project for plant people and cat lovers.

MATERIALS

White cotton fabric: 8″ × 8″ (20.3 × 20.4cm)

Embroidery hoop: 6″ (15.2cm)

Embroidery needle: Size 3 or size 5

6-Stranded Embroidery Floss in the following colors:

A: Light Green (DMC 3819)

B: Green (DMC 704)

C: Dark Green (DMC 906)

D: Aqua (DMC 964)

E: Dark Pink (DMC 352)

F: Pink (DMC 353)

G: Red (DMC 351)

STITCHES

1: Split Stitch

2: Straight Stitch

3: Back Stitch

4: Satin Stitch

5: Lazy Daisy

6: French Knot

Instructions

1. Trace the pattern onto the cotton fabric using your preferred method.

2. Stretch the fabric in the embroidery hoop.

3. Outline the cat with 3 strands of split stitch in Dark Green.

4. Backstitch the shadow around the base of the cat. Backstitch the grass (2 strands).

5. Stitch the plant details on the cat with 2 strands, following the stitch guide. Stitch over the outline of the body where necessary. Satin stitch the ears, mushroom, and leaves. Use French knots for the dots and lazy daisies for the petals as directed.

FEATHERED IN FLOWERS

By Carley Pettitt

Finished Project: 6″ × 6″ (15.2 × 15.2cm)

Stitched Area: 5½″ × 3½″ (14 × 8.9cm)

I grew up with a grandfather whose hobby was carving duck decoys, so mallards are often on my mind. This sampler design celebrates his passion for waterfowl and my own passion for animal conservation and stitching. The goal of this sampler is to allow you to nibble on different stitches at your leisure. Feel like doing some lazy daisies? There's a spot for that. How about a little satin stitch? There's a spot for that, too!

MATERIALS

Quilting cotton or linen: 8″ × 8″ (20.3 × 20.4cm) Kona cotton in Water by Robert Kaufman Fabrics

Wooden embroidery hoop: 6″ (15.2cm) Elbesee

Embroidery needle: Size 7

6-Stranded Embroidery Floss in the following colors:

A: White (DMC BLANC)

B: Black (DMC 310)

C: Cream (DMC 712)

D: Dark Brown (DMC 3371)

E: Mocha Brown (DMC 433)

F: Caramel (DMC 437)

G: Grey (DMC 4125)

H: Yellow (DMC 726)

I: Turquoise (DMC 3814)

J: Teal (DMC 3765)

K: Dark Blue Green (DMC 803)

STITCHES (3 STRANDS)

1: Back Stitch

2: Buttonhole Wheel Stitch

3: Eyelet Stitch

4: Fishbone Stitch

5: French Knot

6: Lazy Daisy

7: Rhodes Stitch

8: Satin Stitch

9: Stem Stitch

10: Straight Stitch

11: Woven Wheel Stitch

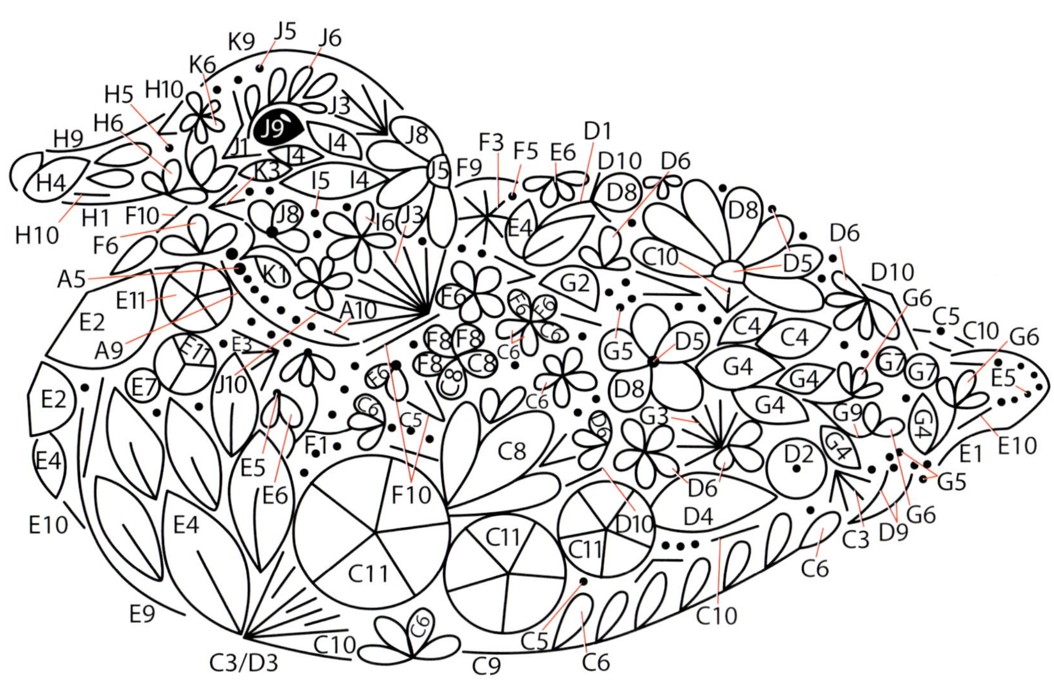

Instructions

1. Trace the pattern onto the fabric using your preferred method. Place the fabric into the hoop. Make sure the pattern is centered and the fabric is tight and wrinkle-free.

2. Stitch the design by starting with your favorite (or, if it's your style, your least favorite) stitch. Stitch the pattern by color block, following the stitch guide as you go.

For example, stitch the yellow (H) beak using stitch types 1, 5, 6, 9, and 10. Then, move onto the Dark Blue Green (K) section with stitch types 1, 3, 6, and 9. I suggest leaving the woven wheels for last so they don't get in the way of completing the stitches around them. Once you've finished stitching the partial buttonhole wheels, use a straight stitch to complete the shape.

3. To stitch the eye, use satin stitch and black (B) to fill the shape. Add a tiny white (A) straight stitch in the top right corner to create a reflection.

4. If necessary, remove any tracing lines or wash the piece. Then, re-stretch the piece in the hoop while it is still damp to prevent any wrinkles or puckering.

SUNNY DAYS

By Anne Oliver of Lolli and Grace

Finished Project: 8″ × 8″ (20.3 × 20.3cm)

Stitched Area: 8″ × 8″ (20.3 × 20.3cm)

With its cheerful colors and white accents, this sunny hoop design is the perfect way to explore basic stitches and try out new techniques. The sun's face features decorative lines, curves, and dots, creating a charming focal point, while the alternating rays are packed with a variety of stitches, from straight lines to interesting motifs used as fillers. As you stitch, you'll build your skills and create a vibrant piece of decor that radiates sunshine and creativity.

MATERIALS

100% cotton fabric: 12″ × 12″ (30.5 × 30.5cm) Kona cotton in Bright Pink by Robert Kaufman Fabrics

White polyester felt: 9″× 9″ (22.9 × 22.9cm) square for backing

White mini pom-pom trim: 1 yard

Wooden embroidery hoop for stitching: 9″ (22.9cm)

Wooden embroidery hoop for display: 8″ (20.3cm)

Embroidery needle: Size 24 chenille

White graphite paper

White gel pen

Ball point pen (preferably red or non-black)

White tacky glue

6-Stranded Embroidery Floss in the following colors:

A: White (DMC Blanc)

B: Bright Yellow (DMC 742)

C: Light Orange (DMC 741)

D: Medium Orange (DMC 947)

E: Dark Orange (DMC 606)

STITCHES

1: Split back stitch

2: Daisy stitch

3: Straight stitch

4: French knot

5: Couching

6: Fan stitch

7: Cable chain stitch

8: Colonial knot

9: Fly stitch

10: Star eyelet

11: Heavy chain stitch

12: Detached wheatear stitch

13: Coral stitch

14: Ermine stitch

15: Palestrina knot stitch

16: Chain stitch twisted

17: Reverse chain stitch

18: Scalloped buttonhole stitch

19: Running stitch

20: Whip stitch

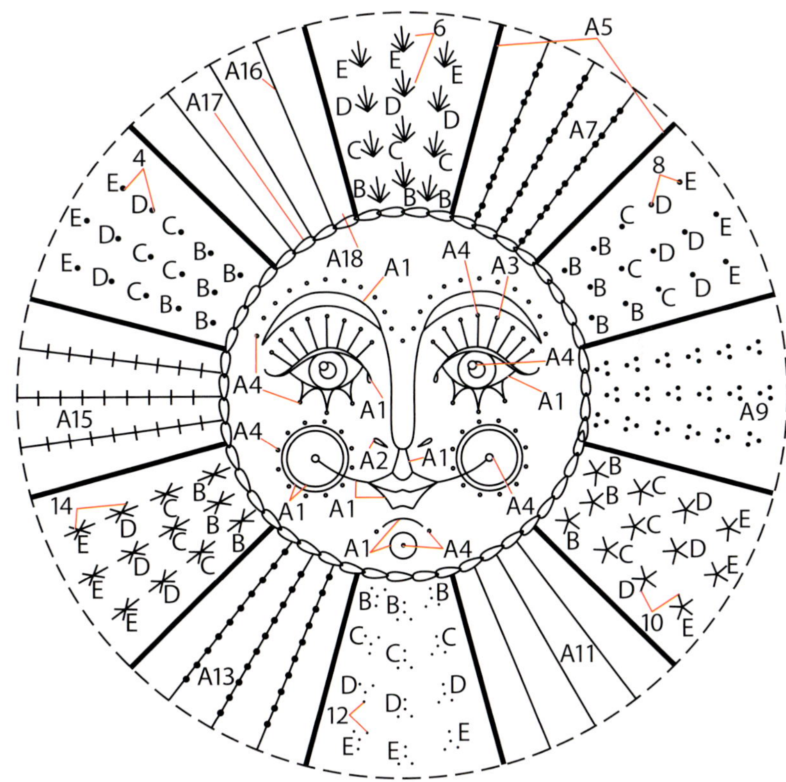

Enlarge 200% to use as template.

Instructions

PREPARATION

1. Stretch the fabric in the 9″ (22.9cm) hoop. Stitch this design in the larger hoop and then transfer it to the 8″ (20.3cm) hoop for display.

2. Cut a circle of white graphite paper that is a little larger than 8″ (20.3cm). Flip the 9″ (22.9cm) hoop over so the stretched fabric is flat against your work surface. Place the white graphite paper onto the fabric so the graphite side is down. With the design facing up, place the pattern on top of the white graphite paper and tape it in place on the fabric. Trace the pattern with the red ball point pen.

3. Remove the pattern and the graphite paper. Use the white gel pen to go over the graphite lines so you can see them more easily as you are stitching. You can leave the fabric stretched in the hoop as it is (called *stitching in the well*) or you can take out the fabric and re-stretch it in the hoop so the traced design is facing up.

STITCHING

Use 3 strands of thread for all sun ray stitches. Use 2 strands of thread for stitching the sun's face. Use 3 strands of thread for the reverse chain stitch and scalloped buttonholes around the sun's face.

1. Stitch the face in white thread following the stitch guide. Use small stitches for the tight curves. Stitch the French knots last.

2. Couch the lines to outline each of the rays (A5 lines on the stitch guide). Use 6 strands of thread for the surface thread (the thread that sits on top of the fabric). Use 1 strand for the couching thread.

> **NOTE**
> Extend all the lines coming out from the central circle past the edge of the pattern so they will go beyond the edge of the display hoop.

3. Fill each ray following the stitch guide.

4. Reverse chain stitch the circle outlining the face. Use 4 stitches per each ray width.

5. Stitch the scalloped buttonholes. Bring the thread up through the top of a chain stitch, then make 5 raised buttonhole stitches inside of each chain using only the outside leg of the chain when you bring the needle under the thread for each stitch. Pull the first buttonhole stitch tight against the thread, make the second looser, and the third very loose. Then, mirror the same tightness for the next two stitches (stitches 2/4 and 1/5 should be the same tightness). After the fifth stitch, go back down through the fabric to anchor the stitches.

Finishing

1. Remove the stitched fabric from the 9″ (22.9cm) hoop and re-stretch it in the 8″ (20.3cm) hoop, being careful to stretch it evenly so the circle of the face doesn't get distorted.

2. Trim the edges of the fabric around the hoop, leaving about 1″ (2.5cm).

3. Cut a long length of any color of thread, and tie a large knot in the end. Running stitch all the way around the edge of the fabric and pull the thread to gather the excess fabric to the back of the hoop. Securely tie off the thread.

4. Remove the outside hoop, and lay the stitched fabric/hoop onto the polyester felt. Trace around the edge of the hoop. Cut ⅛″ (3mm) smaller than the traced line. Place this felt on the back of your hoop and pin it in place. Use two strands of white thread to whip stitch the felt to the edge of the gathered fabric.

5. Use the white tacky glue to attach the mini pom-pom trim around the edge of the hoop.

ABSTRACT ROSE

By Jennifer Davidson of Bloom and Floss

Finished Project: 5˝ (12.7cm) hoop

Stitched Area: approximately 4˝ × 4˝ (10.2 × 10.2cm)

This abstract rose sampler incorporates a variety of colors and techniques, resulting in a vibrant textured artwork. Feel free to experiment with your own color palette and favorite stitches to create something uniquely yours.

MATERIALS

Woven Fabric: 7˝ × 7˝ (18 × 18cm) natural color linen

Wooden embroidery hoop: 5˝ (12.7cm)

Embroidery needle: DMC Size 3

6-Stranded Embroidery Floss in the following colors:

A: Light green (DMC 733)

B: Dark green (DMC 730)

C: Dark gold (DMC 780)

D: Gold (DMC 783)

E: Dark pink (DMC 3805)

F: Medium pink (DMC 3716)

G: Pink (DMC 963)

H: Light pink (DMC 819)

I: Dark blue (DMC 3809)

J: Light blue (DMC 598)

STITCHES (6 STRANDS)

1: French knot

2: Chain stitch

3: Couching

4: Lazy daisy

5: Split backstitch

6: Satin stitch

7: Backstitch (brick stitch)

8: Trellis (3 strands)

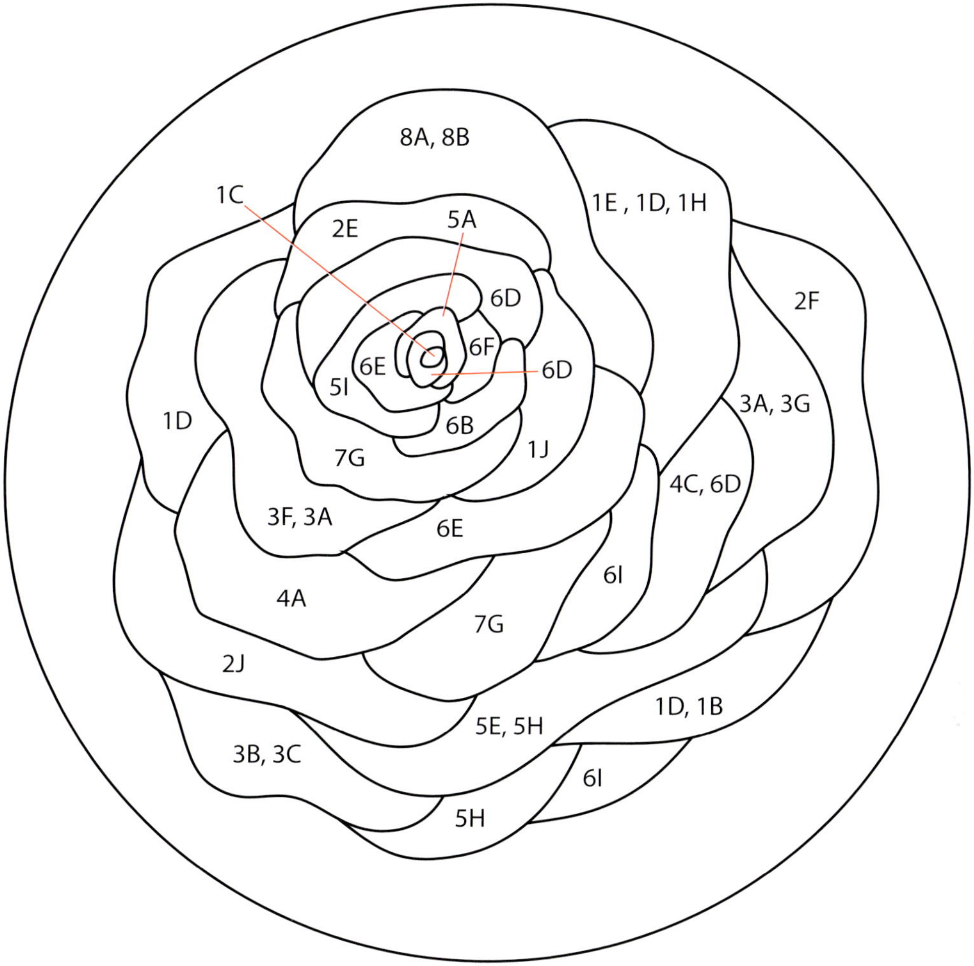

8A, 8B
1C
2E
5A
1E , 1D, 1H
6D
2F
6F
6E
6D
5I
1D
6B
3A, 3G
7G
1J
4C, 6D
3F, 3A
6E
6I
4A
7G
2J
1D, 1B
5E, 5H
3B, 3C
6I
5H

Instructions

1. Trace the template onto the fabric. Insert the fabric in the hoop, ensuring it is drum tight.

2. Following the stitch guide, begin stitching at the center of the rose. Create a single French knot, wrapping the needle twice. Continue working outward from the center as you fill each section, following these guidelines:

- Use 3 strands for the section marked 8A, 8B. Use 733 for the grid lines of the trellis and 730 for the diagonal stitches at each intersection.
- In the section marked 3F, 3A, first fill the section with 3716 satin stitches. Then, place random 733 couching stitches for the basketweave effect.
- In the sections marked 1J and 1D, wrap the needle 3 times for each French knot.
- In the 4A section, stitch 2 horizontal rows of lazy daisy stitches.
- In the 4C and 6D sections, fill with 780 lazy daisy stitches, then fill the centers of each stitch with 783 satin stitches.
- For the section marked 5E, 5H, combine 3 strands of 3805 and 3 strands of 819 before split backstitching.
- In the section marked 3A, 3G, fill with 733 satin stitches, then place random 963 couching stitches for the basketweave effect.
- In the section marked 3B, 3C, fill with 730 satin stitches, then place random 780 couching stitches for the basketweave effect.

VINTAGE INSPIRED SQUARE

By Christen Brown

Finished Project Size:

8″ × 8″ (20.3 × 20.3cm)

Stitched Area: 6¼″ × 6¼″ (15.9 × 15.9cm)

Many years ago, I visited the Museum of International Folk Art in Santa Fe, New Mexico, and was intrigued by an exhibit of embroidered samplers. The simplicity of working the stitches in lines, grids, squares, and rectangles seemed comforting as well as beautiful. Thank you to those who have gone before us, and those that will continue this work after we are gone.

MATERIALS

Cotton or linen fabric: 10″ × 10″ (25.4 × 25.4cm) square in a neutral color

Pellon Shapeflex interfacing: 10″ × 10″ (25.4 × 25.4cm) square

Timtex interfacing: 8″ × 8″ (20.3 × 20.3cm) square

Batting: 8″ × 8″ (20.3 × 20.3cm) square

Felt: 7¾″ × 7¾″ (19.7 × 19.7cm) square

⅜″ (1cm)-wide ribbon: 4″ (10.2cm)

Quilter's ruler: 18″ (45.7cm)

Embroidery needles: Size 2 crewel and small sharps

Scissors: fabric and embroidery

Air erasable pen

Neutral sewing thread

Tacky glue

Sewing machine (optional)

Perle Cotton in the following colors:

A: Medium shell pink (Finca 1975)

B: Light hazel brown (DMC 422)

C: Medium shell gray (Finca 8742)

D: Gray green (Anchor 850)

E: Medium khaki green (Finca 5229)

F: Light shell pink (DMC 223)

G: Medium antique violet (Finca 8620)

H: Off-White (DMC ECRU)

6-Stranded Embroidery Floss in the following colors:

I: Gray green light (DMC 927)

J: Shell pink (DMC 224)

K: Very light tan (DMC 738)

L: Medium shell pink (DMC 152)

M: Off-White (DMC ECRU)

N: Khaki green (DMC 3013)

STITCHES

1: Spiderweb rose stitch

2: Pair of 2 lazy daisy stitches

3: 3-wrap French knot

4: Chain stitch feathered

5: Pistil stitch

6: 2-wrap French knot

7: Coral stitch

8: Crossed lazy daisy stitch

9: Blanket stitch with loose knot stitch

10: Group of 3 lazy daisy stitches

11: Fly stitch stacked

12: Group of 3, 3-wrap French knots

13: Chevron stitch

14: Russian chain stitch

15: Feather stitch single

16: Lazy daisy piggyback stitch

17: Fly stitch

18: Herringbone stitch

19: Straight stitch

20: Lazy daisy stitch

21: Feather stitch

22: Cross stitch

23: Cretan stitch

24: Lazy daisy tulip stitch

25: Pair of 2, 3-wrap French knots

26: Fern stitch modern

27: Lazy daisy with French knot

28: Chain stitch

10M
22B
19C
28C
3M
2E
1AL
17N
5N
21D
2A
19G
19G
10M
18C
20L
19K
3K
27I
26G
15A
13B
11G
10H
3H
9E
6L
16G
14D
8FDK
10M
5I
6G
17N
6J
4B
17C
3J
6C
3N
28C
2E
1AL
3M
24H
25J
7C
23E
2F
3M
2E
1AL

Instructions

1. Following the manufacturer's directions, iron the 10″ × 10″ (25.4 × 25.4cm) square of Shapeflex to the wrong side of the 10″ × 10″ (25.4 × 25.4cm) square of fabric. Machine- or hand-stitch a basting stitch around the raw edges.

2. With an air-erasable pen, draw a line vertically down the center of the fabric. Draw 3 additional lines, 1″ (2.5cm) apart, on either side of this center line. Repeat, drawing horizontally to create a grid.

3. Machine- or hand-stitch over these lines with the sewing thread.

4. Transfer the pattern to the grid using your preferred method.

STITCHING

Following the stitch guide, begin in the center of the square. Move outward, and stitch each row of designs as indicated.

Finishing

1. Place the batting on one side of the Timtex. Layer the wrong side of the embroidered fabric onto the batting. Press the vertical edges to the wrong side of the Timtex. Then, press the horizontal edges to the wrong side.

2. Hand-stitch the raw edges of fabric to the Timtex.

3. Fold the ribbon in half. Glue or hand-stitch the raw edges onto the fabric back at the top of the piece to create a hanging loop.

4. Glue or hand-stitch the felt to the back.

HOOP SAMPLER

By Christen Brown

Finished Project Size:

6″ × 6″ (15.2 × 15.2cm) hoop

Stitched Area: 6″ × 6″ (15.2 × 15.2cm)

This fun project displays a delightful array of embroidery stitches worked on a cotton base in size 8 perle cotton thread. I chose stitches that could be easily worked along a curve, including the feather stitch, blanket stitch, chain stitch and variations. This is a great way to exercise your creative embroidery skills!

MATERIALS

Green cotton fabric: 9″ × 9″ (22.9 × 22.9cm) square

Pellon Shapeflex interfacing: 9″ × 9″ (22.9 × 22.9cm) square

Felt: 6″ (15.2cm) circle

⅜″ (1cm)-wide ribbon (optional): 4″ (10.2cm) suggested if you do not buy a hoop with metal hanger

Embroidery hoop: 6″ (15.2cm) wooden, or faux wood rubber with metal hanger

Embroidery needles: Size 2 crewel and small sharps

Scissors: fabric and embroidery

Quilter's ruler: 18″ (45.7cm)

Artist's Loft Small & Large Circle Template (optional): Size 1⁄16″ to 2¼″

Air erasable pen

Sewing thread

Rotary cutter and mat

Tacky Glue

Sewing machine (optional)

Perle Cotton in the following colors:

A: Dark mauve (Finca 2240)

B: Medium shell pink (Finca 1975)

C: Emerald green (Finca 4350)

D: Very light pistachio (DMC 369)

E: Medium lavender (Finca 2699)

F: Very light violet (Anchor 95)

G: Pale yellow (DMC 144)

H: Light yellow (Finca 1214)

I: Peacock blue (Finca 3560)

STITCHES

1: Feather stitch

2: 2-wrap French knot

3: Chain stitch cable

4: Blanket stitch looped

5: Pistil stitch

6: Stem stitch

7: French knot stitch flower—6 petals

8: Chain stitch open

9: Group of 3 lazy daisy stitches

10: Straight stitch

11: Blanket stitch

12: Fly stitch stacked

13: 3-wrap French knot

14: Chain stitch double

15: Feather stitch single

16: Bell flower stitch

17: Lazy daisy stitch

18: Chain stitch

19: Looped tendril stitch

20: Group of 3, 3-wrap French knots

Instructions

PREPARATION

1. Following the manufacturer's directions, iron the 9″ × 9″ (22.9 × 22.9cm) square of Shapeflex to the wrong side of the 9″ × 9″ (22.9 × 22.9cm) square of fabric.

2. Machine- or hand-stitch a basting stitch around the raw edges.

3. With an air-erasable pen, draw a 6″ (15.2cm) circle in the center of the fabric. Stitch this line with a basting stitch and sewing thread.

4. Transfer the pattern to the fabric using your preferred method. You can also draw 2¼″ (5.7cm), 1¾″ (4.4cm), 1¼″ (3.1cm), and ¾″ (1.9cm) circles to match the pattern.

20A
13C
12B
2D
10D
2H
13B
11E
9B
8C
4F
3D
19F
13E
18I
2C
5I
6G
2D
7A
9G
14E
15B
2H
2C
1A
2G
6C
16D
2E
17H

STITCHING

Follow the stitch guide to embroider the circles. Save 20A and 13B for last. Incorporate the following notes:

- For loop 4F in the center circle, work the base of the blanket stitch looped on the ¾″ (1.9cm) circle. Work the tops on the 1¼″ (3.1cm) circle.
- For loop 6G in the center circle, work the stem stitch under the base of the blanket stitch.
- For the 9B and 2H loops in the top left and bottom right circles, stitch 3 lazy daisy stitches grouped around the circle. Add one 2-wrap French knot in each lazy daisy group and between each group.
- For the 11E loop in the top left and bottom right circles, stitch the base of the blanket stitch on the 1¼″ (3.1cm) circle and the tips on the ¾″ (1.9cm) circle.
- For the 15B loop in the top right and bottom left, work the feather stitch base on the 1¾″ (4.4cm) circle with the tips toward the 1¼″ (3.1cm) circle.
- For the 16D loop in the top right and bottom left, work the outer edge of the bell flower stitch on the ¾″ (1.9cm) circle and the center on the edge of the 6″ (15.2cm) circle.
- For 19F in the 4 smallest circles, stitch 1 looped tendril stitch on each spoke.
- For 9G and 2D in the 4 smallest circles, work 1 group of 3 lazy daisy stitches between each looped tendril stitch. Work one 2-wrap French knot in each lazy daisy group and between each group.

Finishing

1. Add a 2″ (5.1cm) seam allowance to the outer edge of the 6″ (15.2cm) circle. Cut along the line with scissors.

2. Machine-or hand-stitch around the raw edges of the fabric ¼″ (6mm) from the raw edges.

3. Place the fabric in the embroidery hoop and tighten.

4. Thread a small sharps needle with sewing thread, doubled. Knot the tail. Fold under the raw edges of fabric at the ¼″ (6mm) stitch line. Running stitch along the folded edges.

5. Gently pull the thread to gather the stitches and fabric. Anchor-knot the thread into the folded edges. Cut the thread.

Optional: Fold the ribbon in half. Glue or hand-stitch the raw edges onto the fabric back to create a hanging loop.

6. Cut a 6″ (15.2cm) circle of felt. Glue or hand-stitch this to the back of the piece.

TEACUP

By Theresa Lawson

Finished Project: 6″ × 6″ (15.2 × 15.2cm)

Stitched Area: 4¾″ × 4½″ (12.1 × 11.4cm)

This elegant little teacup sampler will have you wishing for cucumber sandwiches, scones and fancy doilies. It's filled with exciting embroidery techniques you may not have used before. Some stitches are even combined to create the patterns fit for an elegant luncheon. Finish your piece off with the quirky little teabag tag. All the colors in this pattern can be substituted for your favorite colors.

MATERIALS

Linen fabric: 8″ × 8″ (20.3 × 20.3cm) natural flax or cotton linen blend

Quilting cotton fabric: 2 squares 4″ × 4″ (10.2 × 10.2cm)

White felt (optional): 1″ × 1″ square (2.5 × 2.5cm) for padding teabag tag

Embroidery hoop: 6″ (15.2cm)

Embroidery hoop (optional): 2″ (5cm)

Embroidery needle: Size 8 crewel

Mirror or reflective cardboard sheet

6-Stranded Embroidery Floss in the following colors:

Teacup

Outline: Black floss (DMC BLANC)

A: White floss

B: Medium grey floss (DMC 318)

C: Lime green floss (DMC 166)

D: Dark pink floss (DMC 3801)

E: Medium blue floss (DMC 3843)

F: Medium purple floss (DMC 552)

G: Light pink floss (DMC 957)

H: Medium green floss (DMC 905)

I: Medium-light green floss (DMC 907)

J: Light yellow floss (DMC 727)

K: Medium yellow (DMC 973)

L: Metallic gold thread (DMC E3852)

M: Light brown floss (DMC 738)

N: Light grey floss (DMC 3024)

O: Brown floss (DMC 420)

P: Orange floss (DMC 970)

Teabag Tag

A: White sewing thread

B: Medium yellow floss (DMC 973)

C: Dark blue floss (DMC 797)

D: Variegated size 8 perle cotton (any color)

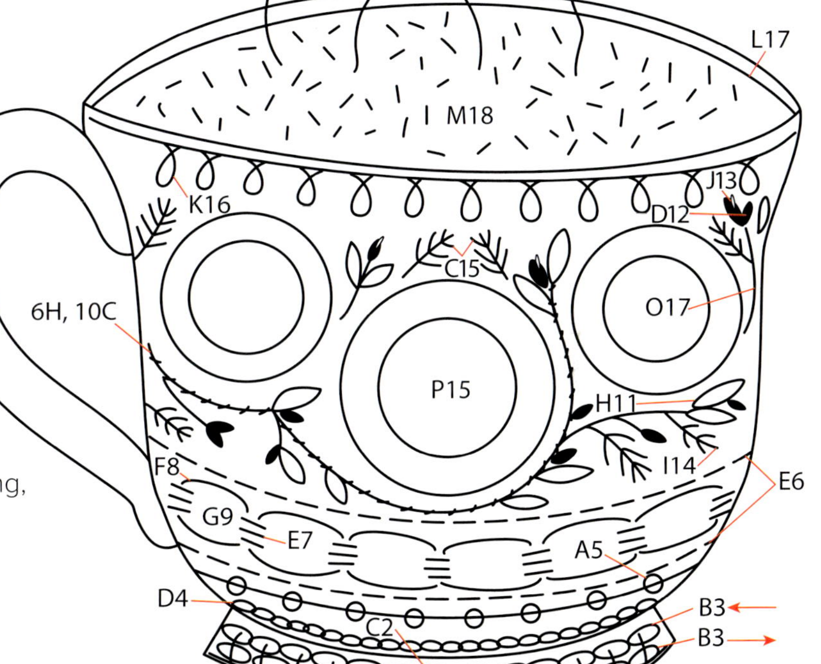

STITCHES

Teacup

1: Padded satin stitch (3 strands for padding, 2 strands for satin stitch)

2: Blanket stitch (4 strands)

3: Chain stitch (3 strands)

4: Split stitch (6 strands)

5: Palestrina knot (6 strands)

6: Backstitch (4 strands)

7: Straight stitch (4 strands)

8: Weave (4 strands)

9: French knot (4 strands)

10: Whip stitch (4 strands)

11: Detached chain stitch (4 strands)

12: Granitos stitch (6 strands)

13: Seed stitch (6 strands)

14: Fishbone stitch (4 strands)

15: Shisha embroidery (6 strands)

16: Basque stitch (3 strands)

17: Stem stitch (3 strands)

18: Seed stitch (4 strands)

Teabag Tag

1: Backstitch (sewing thread)

2: Whip stitch (sewing thread)

3: Blanket stitch (6 strands)

Instructions

PREPARATION

Trace the pattern onto the linen or linen blend fabric using your preferred method. Load it into the hoop, and stretch the fabric tight.

STITCHING

1. Outline the cup (excluding the handle) using backstitch and black floss. Use padded satin stitch to fill the cup handle in white floss (A). Outline the handle with backstitch and black floss.

2. Start filling the bottom of the cup. Add 2 lines of chain stitches to the B3 area, working each line in an opposite direction (one line from left to right, and the other right to left).

3. Blanket stitch from left to right on top of the chain stitches with 4 strands of lime green. Finish each stitch through the holes in the top row of chain stitches.

4. Using all 6 strands of dark pink floss, split stitch a line along the bottom of the cup's bowl. Above the pink split stitch, use all 6 strands of white floss to create a Palestrina knot line. Above that, backstitch a line with 4 strands of medium blue. Approximately ½″ (1.2cm) above, backstitch another line in the same color.

5. In between the 2 medium blue lines, stitch groups of 3 stacked straight stitches in the same color. Stitch them ½″ (1.2cm) apart.

6. Use 4 strands of medium purple to weave up and down through the blue straight stitches. Repeat going back the other direction. Stitch down through the fabric and the beginning and end of each line. Stitch a 4-strand light pink French knot in each oval.

7. Follow the stitch guide to fill in the greenery around the circles. You don't have to follow the pattern exactly, so feel free to add extra flower or leaves to fill gaps. Backstitch the vines, then whipstitch around each stitch. Use detached chain stitch and fishbone stitch for the leaves. Stem stitch the brown twigs.

8. To stitch the flowers, use 6 strands of dark pink floss and granitos stitch. Vary the size of the flowers. Seed stitch 1 small light yellow center on each large flower with 6 strands.

9. Basque stitch the rim of the cup. If you prefer, you can use a trusted chain or chain stitch.

10. Cut 3 circles of mirrored cardboard using the inner circle of the pattern. If you prefer, you can replace the cardboard with patterned paper, photographs, or fabric.

11. Stitch the circles in place with 6 strands of orange and shisha stitch.

12. Stem stitch the metallic gold thread to the back rim of the cup, then seed stitch the interior of the cup with light brown. If you prefer green tea or matcha, change the color to light green!

13. Stem stitch the steam with 3 strands of light grey.

TAG STITCHING

1. Place the felt square (if using) on the wrong side of 1 of the 4″ × 4″ (10.2 × 10.2cm) pieces of fabric. Stitch the word *TEA* to the right side of the fabric, securing the felt to the fabric. If necessary, use the mini hoop for tension, or stitch loosely without a hoop.

2. Place the remaining piece of fabric right sides together with the Step 1 fabric. Following the tea bag pattern, backstitch the tag shape through both pieces of fabric. Leave the top of the bag open. Use the mini hoop if desired.

3. Cut out the tag shape following the pattern. Push the tea bag right side out through the gap. Close the gap with whip stitches, tucking under the raw edges.

4. Blanket stitch around the tag with 6 strands of medium yellow floss. Cut a 6″ (15.2cm) length of variegated perle cotton and tie a knot in one end. From back to front, pull the string through the top of the tag. Secure it to the inside of the teacup just over the rim.

5. Use your favorite finishing technique to tidy the back of the embroidery hoop or set it into your preferred frame.

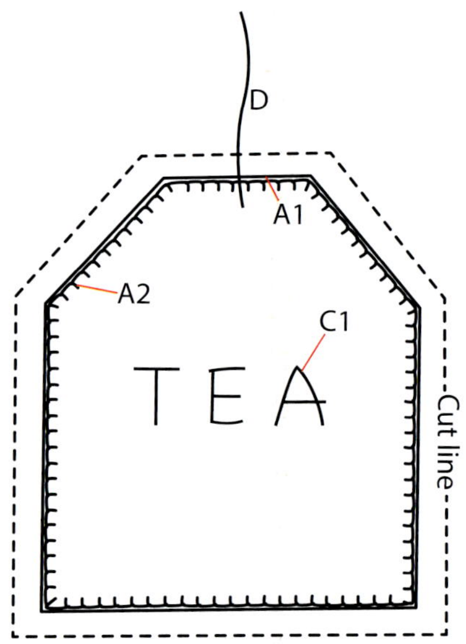

TEA

MOUNTAINS AND FIELDS

By Melissa Galbraith

Finished Project: 5″ (12.7cm) circle

Stitched Area: 4½″ × 3½″ (11.4 × 8.8cm)

I love taking long walks with my pups around the neighborhood. On a clear day, you can see a beautiful mountain view. This sampler was inspired by those views and the Pacific Northwest. I hope you enjoy creating a textural landscape and exploring nine different embroidery stitches.

MATERIALS

Fabric: 7″ × 7″ (17.7 × 17.7cm) pink spotted batik

Wooden embroidery hoop: 5″ (12.7cm) Nurge No. 2

Embroidery needle: Size 5 sharp

Transfer pen

Embroidery scissors

6-Stranded Embroidery Floss in the following colors:

A: Silver (DMC 01)

B: Grey (DMC 03)

C: Medium grey (DMC 414)

D: Dark grey with metallic flecks (DMC Etoile 3799)

E: Light mauve (DMC 152)

F: Bright dark green (DMC 3345)

G: Medium dark green (DMC 937)

H: Medium green (DMC 470)

I: Pale green (DMC 3348)

J: Golden green (DMC 833)

K: Bright avocado green (DMC 581)

L: Dark olive green (DMC 3051)

STITCHES

1: Satin stitch (2 strands)

2: Long and short stitch (3 strands)

3: Seed stitch (4 strands)

4: Detached chain/lazy daisy stitch (4 strands)

5: Reverse chain stitch (4 strands)

6: Split backstitch (3 strands)

7: Couching (6 strands and 2 strands)

8: French knot (3 strands)

9: Connected fly stitch (2 strands)

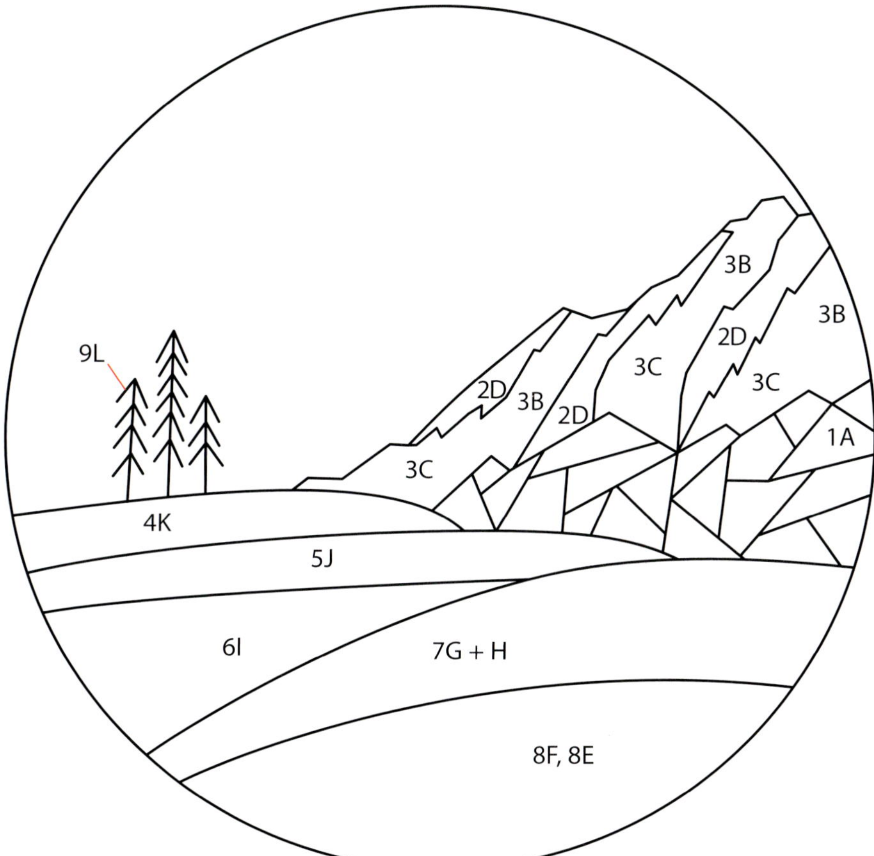

Instructions

PREPARATION

Transfer the pattern to the fabric using your preferred method. Place the fabric into the embroidery hoop and tighten.

STITCHING

1. Use 2 strands of 01 to satin stitch the lowest section of the mountain. For each section, change the direction of the satin stitch.

2. Use 3 strands of 3799 to vertically long and short stitch the dark crevices of the taller mountain, following the angle of each shape.

3. Use 4 strands of 414 to densely seed stitch the lower sections of the mountain between the crevices. Repeat with 03 to fill the upper sections.

4. Use 581 to vertically lazy daisy stitch the top left of the field.

5. Follow the stitch guide to fill the rest of the field. Use parallel horizontal rows in the 5J section. Use horizontal rows that follow the shape of the 6I section.

6. For the 7G+H section, use 6 strands of 937 for the laying thread and 2 strands of 470 for the couching thread. Start at the top of the section, and following the shape of the area, zigzag the thread in rows.

7. In the last section, first add the 152 French knots as flowers, then densely fill French knots in 3346 for the rest of the space.

8. Fly stitch the trees in 3051. Start at the bottom of the trunk.

9. If needed, remove any pattern marks. Trim the fabric to 1″ (2.5cm) from the outer edge of the hoop. Use a running stitch to gather the fabric along the back of the hoop.

A SLICE OF PIE

By Melissa Galbraith

Finished Project: 5″ (12.7cm) circle

Stitched Area: 4″ (10.2cm) circle

A Slice of Pie was inspired by my love for all things sweet and baked goods. I often can't choose just one dessert and love an assortment. With this sampler, you'll get to explore seventeen different embroidery stitches and six delicious slices of pie. Enjoy!

MATERIALS

White cotton fabric: 7″ × 7″ (17.7 × 17.7cm)

Light brown cotton fabric: 4″ × 4″ (10.2 × 10.2cm) Kona cotton

Wooden embroidery hoop: 5″ (12.7cm) Nurge No. 2

Embroidery needle: Size 5 sharp

Scissors: Embroidery and fabric

Water soluble sticky transfer paper (Sulky Sticky Fabri-Solvy or similar)

Long sewing pin

6-Stranded Embroidery Floss in the following colors:

A: Medium green (DMC 470)

B: Bright green (DMC 166)

C: Dark brown (DMC 938)

D: Medium brown (DMC 780)

E: Light brown (DMC 436)

F: Medium light brown (DMC 435)

G: Red (DMC 816)

H: Medium coral (DMC 351)

I: Dark reddish brown (DMC 3857)

J: Light reddish brown (632)

K: Navy blue (DMC 823)

L: Cobalt blue (DMC 3842)

M: Very light pink (DMC 3770)

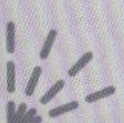

STITCHES

1: Satin stitch (3 strands)

2: Trellis stitch (6 strands)

3: French knot (2 strands)

4: Split back stitch (3 strands)

5: Blanket stitch (3 strands)

6: Danish knot (4 strands)

7: Couching stitch (6+2 strands)

8: Chain stitch (4 strands)

9: Weave stitch (6 strands)

10: Spiral trellis (4 strands)

11: Bullion knots (6 strands)

12: Needle weaving bar (6 strands)

13: Leaf stitch (4 strands)

14: Seed stitch (2 and 3 strands)

15: Back stitch (3 strands)

16: Cast-on stitch (6 strands)

17: Stab stitch (2 strands)

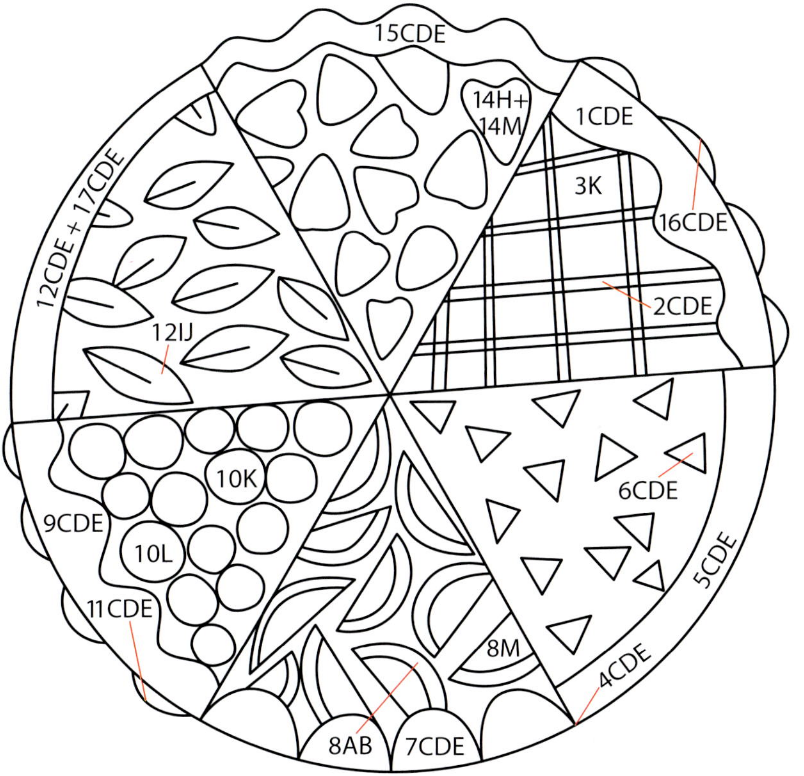

Instructions

PREPARATION

Cut out a 4″ (10.2cm) circle of brown cotton fabric. Trace the pattern onto sticky water soluble transfer paper. Peel off the backing, then align the right side of the brown fabric with the circle of the pie, and stick the pattern paper. Baste the design to the base cotton fabric (white). Stretch the fabric in the 5″ (12.7cm) hoop.

STITCHING

Crust

1. Hold 1 strand each of 938, 436, and 780 (CDE) for the crust. Split backstitch the divider line between each slice.

2. Start with the cherry pie crust. Use 3 stitches for each trellis line, then use satin stitch to fill the crust. Along the outer edge, add 4 evenly spaced out cast-on stitches.

3. Blanket stitch the crust on the chocolate cream slice with the loop facing the outer edge of the pie.

4. Couching stitch spirals for the crust of the apple slice. Use 2 strands of 436 for the couching stitches. Use 2 strands of each color (CDE) for the laying thread. Start on the outside and work toward the center.

5. Weave stitch the crust of the blueberry slice. Stitch the vertical stitches, then weave horizontally. Add 4 spaced out bullion knots along the edge.

6. Use the needle weaving bar to create the crust for the pecan slice. Start the needle weaving bar at one end of the pie crust. When the bar is complete, tack the end down at the other side of the pie crust. Then tack the bar down along the outer edge of the pie with stab stitches.

7. Fill in the strawberry pie crust with a wavy back stitch.

Pie Fillings

1. Use 938 and Danish knots to add chocolate chips to the chocolate cream slice.

2. Use 2 strands each of 632 and 3857 to leaf stitch the pecans for the pecan slice.

3. Fill in half of the blueberry circles using 3842 and spiral trellis. Fill in the other circles with 823 and spiral trellis.

4. Chain stitch the apple skin with 470 and 166. Chain stitch the apple flesh with 3770, starting closest to the skins.

5. Use 2 strands of 816 to densely fill French knots for the cherry slice.

6. Seed stitch 351 to densely fill the strawberry shapes. Seed stitch seeds on top with 3770.

Finishing

1. Remove the embroidery from the hoop. Using warm water, gently rinse away the water soluble stabilizer paper. Let the fabric lay flat to dry. Then, replace the embroidery in the hoop.

2. Trim the fabric to 1″ (2.5cm) from the outer edge. Running stitch along the edge to gather the fabric to the back of the hoop.

NATIVITY SCENE CHRISTMAS ORNAMENT

By Stella Caraman

Finished Size: 4″ × 2⅝″ (10.2 × 6.7cm)

Stitched Area: 4″ × 2⅝″ (10.2 × 6.7cm)

This ornament is a beautiful reminder of the Christmas story, designed to bring warmth and joy to your holiday season. It offers an opportunity to slow down, embrace mindfulness, and enjoy a peaceful crafting project in the lead-up to Christmas. This pattern is ideal for intermediate embroiderers or adventurous beginners.

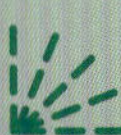

MATERIALS

Medium-weight woven fabric: 10″ × 8″ (25 × 21cm) unbleached 100% cotton calico

Wooden embroidery hoop: 6″ (15.2cm)

Embroidery needle: Size 24 cross stitch or size 7 sharp point

Matching color basic sewing thread

Poly-fiber fill

Plastic beads for filling

3mm-wide cotton twisted cord

6-Stranded Embroidery Floss in the following colors:

A: White (DMC B5200)

B: Yellow (DMC 743)

C: Light beige (DMC 644)

D: Medium beige (DMC 422)

E: Brown (DMC 3790)

F: Light aquamarine blue (DMC 503)

G: Teal deep blue-green (DMC 501)

H: Carmine red (DMC 221)

I: Black (DMC 310)

STITCHES

1: Algerian eye stitch (Star Eyelet Stitch) (2 strands)

2: Back stitch (1 and 3 strands)

3: Colonial knot (2 and 3 strands)

4: Cross stitch (2 strands)

5: Long & short stitch with split (3 strands)

6: Rice stitch (2 and 3 strands)

7: Satin stitch (2 and 3 strands)

8: Straight stitch (2 strands)

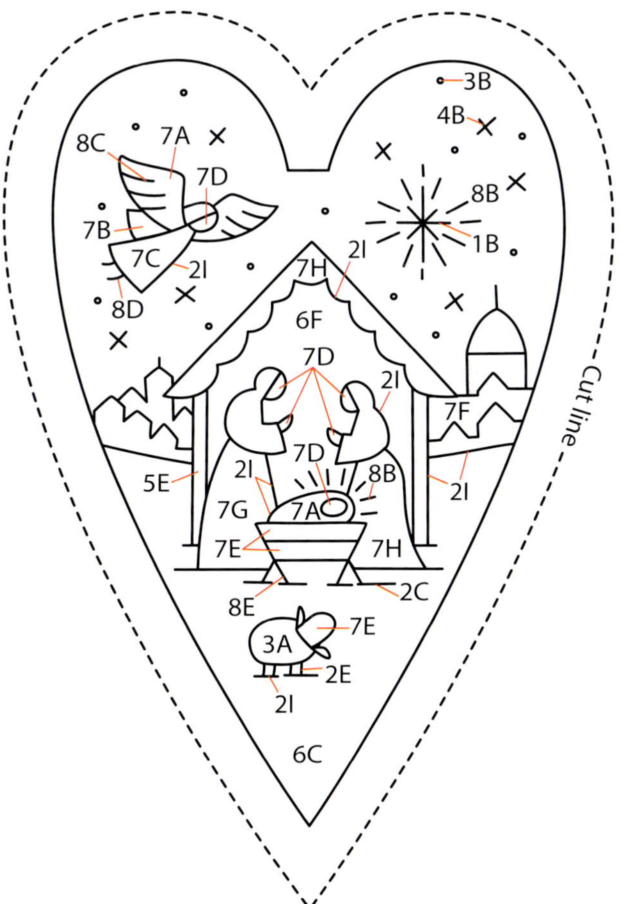

Instructions

PREPARATION

Trace the pattern onto the fabric rectangle using your preferred method (with the rectangle arranged vertically). Offset the design so you can use the rest of the fabric for the back of the ornament, but make sure you can still easily center the design in the hoop.

STITCHING

1. Follow the stitch guide to stitch the manger, then the walls of the stable, both in 3790.

2. Satin stitch the roof in 221, going from the center to each side.

3. Stitch the baby Jesus following the stitch guide. Stitch the face first, then the cloth.

4. Stitch Mary and Joseph, reversing the stitch order (stitch their robes first, then their hands and face) and following the stitch guide.

5. Rice stitch the inside of the stable, scattering the stitches as densely as you prefer.

6. Stitch the head of the sheep, followed by the fur, and then the legs.

7. Embroider the angel wings with B5200, then blend in 644 at the bottoms of the wings. Stitch the robe, then the hair and face following the stitch guide. Finally, stitch the legs.

8. Come back to the baby Jesus to embroider the aura around the head. Then, embroider the star of Bethlehem and rays. Add the stars across the sky, evenly mixing cross stitches and colonial knots.

9. Rice stitch the texture on the ground. Back stitch the base of the sheep, the people, and the manger to give the look of a shadow. Satin stitch the city landscape in the background.

10. Embroider outlines on *some* of the shapes, using back stitch and 1 strand of 310 to subtly differentiate shapes and colors, defining the main figures.

FINISHING

1. Remove the fabric from the hoop. Fold the unstitched part of the fabric behind the embroidered design, wrong sides together. Pin, and then use the pattern to cut out the heart shape (outer solid line).

2. Remove the pins, and turn the heart so the right sides are together. Pin again. Leaving a 1½″ (3.8cm) gap at the bottom right of the heart, back stitch around the heart shape with a ¼″ (6mm) seam allowance. Place the cotton cord in the middle top of the heart, sewing it in between the 2 layers with the loop on the inside and the ends sticking out.

3. Cut into the seam allowance of the heart, going right up to the line of stitching around the whole shape. Turn the shape right side out, pulling the cord from the inside through the gap. Push out all the corners and curves.

NOTE
As needed, remove any marks left from transferring the pattern before continuing to the next step.

4. Fill the ornament with poly fiber, adding small bits into the top of the heart and moving down. Be generous, making a rounded shape. Alternate adding some plastic beads to give the ornament some weight.

5. Close the gap with ladder stitch.

YELLOW MEADOW

By Aliaksandra Dzyachenka

Stitched Area: 5¾″ × 5½″ (14.5 × 14cm)

Wildflowers have always been a symbol of simplicity and harmony in nature for me. St. John's Wort is a symbol of sunshine. Its bright golden-yellow flowers seem to hold a piece of summer light. The round clusters of tansy flowers resemble tiny golden coins gathered in a bouquet. Yarrow has an airy elegance, which brings lightness and grace to any composition.

MATERIALS

Cotton fabric: 11″ × 11″ (27.9 × 27.9cm) Makower Ecru Spectrum 2000-Q53 or Makower Ivory Spectrum 2000-Q02

Wooden embroidery hoop: 6″ (15.2cm)

Embroidery needle: Size 5 sharps

Pilot Frixion pen

6-Stranded Embroidery Floss in the following colors:

A: Dark yellow (DMC 728)

B: Orange-brown (DMC 782)

C: White (DMC 3865)

D: Emerald green (DMC 3362)

E: Pale emerald green (DMC 3363)

F: Green (DMC 936)

G: Dark green (DMC 935)

H: Yellow (DMC 3821)

I: Lemon yellow (DMC 18)

J: Dark beige (DMC 3782)

K: Grassy green (DMC 3364)

STITCHES

1: Stem stitch (1 strand)

2: Satin stitch (2 strands)

3: Straight stitch (1 strand and 4 strands)

4: Pistil stitch (1 strand)

5: Fishbone stitch (1 strand)

6: French knot (1 strand)

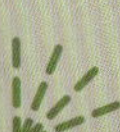

3D
3B
4C
6C
2A
2A
3C
6J
2I
3D
1D
1F, 3F
3F, 3G
1F
5D
2H
5D
1D
5E
1G
5D
1K
5D
1D
1D

Instructions

PREPARATION

Transfer the template to the fabric using your preferred method. I suggest tracing the design with the heat-erasable pen using a light box or window. Place the fabric in the hoop and tighten until it is drum-tight.

STITCHING

St. John's Wort

1. Follow the stitch guide to first stitch the St. John's wort flowers in the center of the piece. Start with the petals, and then add the petal shadows, stamens, and French knot centers. Wrap the thread twice for both the pistil stitches and French knots.

2. Embroider the stalk with stem stitch. Then, stitch the buds and sepals. Finally, stitch the leaves with fishbone stitch.

Yarrow

There are 2 yarrow plants with small star-shaped flowers, one on either side of the St. John's wort.

1. Embroider the stalks with stem stitch. To embroider the leaves, first stem stitch the central veins. Then, add 1-stranded straight stitches extending from the center using both 935 and 936.

2. Embroider the centers of the yarrow flowers with 2-wrap French knots. Then, add the tiny petals around the centers with 4-stranded straight stitches.

Tansy

There are 2 tansy plants with round, oval flowers, one on the left side and one on the right side.

1. Embroider the stalks with stem stitch. Embroider the leaves with fishbone stitch, using 3363 and 3362.

2. Satin stitch the flowers, adding horizontal ovals at the tops of the stems. Use both 3821 and 18. Embroider the sepals with 1-stranded straight stitches.

Finishing

Remove any marks from transferring the pattern, then display as desired in the hoop or a frame.

ills. Some experts say, however, that the name is a reference to
the plant's virginal white flowers.
Once grown commercially as a drug, feverfew is now
regarded as no more than a noxious weed to be rooted out, but it
is very persistent and hard to eradicate. It is especially common
on walls, from where it spreads readily even though its seeds
lack 'parachutes' of hairs to catch the wind.

FLORAL HEART

By Aliaksandra Dzyachenka

Finished Size: 6″ × 6″(15.2 × 15.2cm) hoop

Stitched Area: 4⅜″ × 4⅜″ (11.1 × 11.1cm)

The sheer variety of nature inspired this piece: the bright gold of St. John's wort, the airy lightness of chamomile, the sophistication of white melilot. While I was embroidering this flower heart, I thought about the fragility and resilience of these blooms. They endure all conditions, thriving and sharing their beauty as an integral part of the larger natural world.

MATERIALS

Cotton fabric: 10″ × 10″ (25.4 × 25.4cm) Makower Ecru Spectrum 2000-Q53 or Makower Ivory Spectrum 2000-Q02

Wooden embroidery hoop: 6″ (15.2cm)

Embroidery needle: Size 5 sharps

Pilot Frixion pen

6-Stranded Embroidery Floss in the following colors:

A: Dark yellow (DMC 728)

B: Orange-brown (DMC 782)

C: White (DMC 3865)

D: Emerald green (DMC 3362)

E: Pale emerald green (DMC 3363)

F: Grey green (DMC 3053)

G: Light beige (DMC 822)

H: Dark beige (DMC 3782)

I: Dark green (DMC 3051)

J: Light green (DMC 523)

K: Pale yellow (DMC 3822)

L: Olive green (DMC 3012)

STITCHES

1: Stem stitch (1 strand)

2: Satin stitch (1 strand and 2 strands)

3: Straight stitch (1 strand)

4: Pistil stitch (1 strand)

5: Fishbone stitch (1 strand)

6: French knots (1 strand)

7: Long and short stitch (1 strand and 2 strands)

8: Fly stitch (2 strands)

Instructions

PREPARATION

Transfer the template to the fabric using your preferred method. I suggest tracing the design with the heat-erasable pen using a light box or window. Place the fabric in the hoop and tighten until it is drum-tight.

STITCHING

St. John's Wort

1. Follow the stitch guide to embroider the St. John's wort flowers around the heart. There are 2 clusters: on the bottom left of the heart and the lower right side. Satin stitch the petals with 2 strands, and then add the petal shadows, stamens, and French knot centers. Wrap the thread twice for both the pistil stitches and French knots.

2. Embroider the stalks with stem stitch. Straight stitch the sepals. Satin stitch the buds with 2 strands. Finally, fishbone stitch the leaves.

Chamomile

1. Follow the stitch guide to embroider the chamomile. There are 2 clusters: on the lower left side and the top right curve. Satin stitch the petals with 2 strands, then fill the centers with 3-wrap French knots.

2. Embroider the stalks with stem stitch. Satin stitch the sepals with 1 strand, and straight stitch the buds.

Dwarf Everlasting

1. Follow the stitch guide to embroider the dwarf everlasting. There are 2 clusters: on the top right curve and middle left side. Stitch the stalks with stem stitches and straight stitches. Satin stitch the leaves with 1 strand.

2. Stitch the flowers with densely-packed 3-wrap French knots.

Perennial Ryegrass

1. Follow the stitch guide to embroider the ryegrass. There are 2 stalks: dangling into the center on the right and on the upper left side. Stem stitch the stalk.

2. Embroider the spikelets at the tops of the stalks with angled straight stitches. Embroider the leaves with 1-stranded long and short stitches.

White Clover

1. Follow the stitch guide to embroider the clover. There are 2 clusters: on the bottom right and upper left curve. Long and short stitch the flowers with 2 strands, blending 822, 3782, and 523 (from bottom to top, dark to light).

2. Embroider the stalk with stem stitch. Fly stitch the larger leaves, then add the leaf pattern with straight stitches of different lengths on top. Satin stitch the smaller leaves with 1 strand.

White Melilot

1. Follow the stitch guide to stitch the white melliot. There are 2 clusters: dangling into the center on the left and on the middle right side. Embroider the stalks with stem stitch.

2. Straight stitch the leaves with 1 strand. Straight stitch the petals with 2 strands.

3. Stitch 1-wrap French knots at the tops of the flowers.

Finishing

Remove any marks from transferring the pattern, then display as desired in the hoop or a frame.

a) basal part of the plant
b) culm with spike
c) detail of flowering spikelet
d) detail of flower stalk

FLY AGARIC MUSHROOM

By Aliaksandra Dzyachenka

Finished Size: 4″ × 4″ (10.2 × 10.2cm) hoop

Stitched Area: 3¼″ × 2¾″ (8.3 × 7cm)

An autumn forest is an endless source of inspiration. It is especially beautiful in the early morning, when the rays of the sun break through the yellowed leaves. Soft moss, the cracking of a broken twig under the feet, silence interrupted by bird singing: it's magical. And, the bright red hats of fly agaric underfoot.

MATERIALS

Cotton fabric: 7″ × 7″ (17.8 × 17.8cm) Makower Ecru Spectrum 2000-Q53

Wooden embroidery hoop: 4″ (10.2cm)

Embroidery needle: Size 5 sharps

Pilot Frixion pen

6-Stranded Embroidery Floss in the following colors:

A: Light green (DMC 3051)

B: Swamp green (DMC 3011)

C: Dark green (DMC 935)

D: Dark blue (DMC 3750)

E: Pale blue (DMC 931)

F: White (DMC 3865)

G: Beige (DMC 822)

H: Grey (DMC 640)

I: Pale red (DMC 22)

J: Orange red (DMC 920)

K: Dark red (DMC 3777)

STITCHES

1: Split stitch (1 strand)

2: Long and short stitch (1 strand)

3: Fishbone stitch (1 strand)

4: French knots (1 strand and 2 strands)

5: Stem stitch (1 strand)

6: Straight stitches (1 strand)

7: Turkey rug stitch (6 strands)

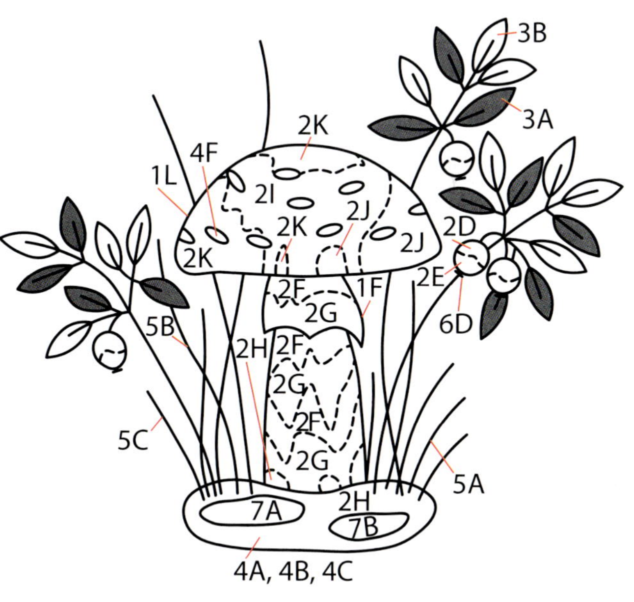
3B
3A
2K
4F
1L
2I
2J
2K
2J
2K
2D
2F
1F
2E
2G
6D
5B
2H
2F
2G
2F
5C
2G
5A
2H
7A
7B
4A, 4B, 4C

Instructions

PREPARATION

Transfer the template to the fabric using your preferred method. I suggest tracing the design with the heat-erasable pen using a light box or window. Place the fabric in the hoop and tighten until it is drum-tight.

STITCHING

Fly Agaric Mushroom

1. Follow the stitch guide to embroider the mushroom. Split stitch the outline of the stem, then fill the sections of the stem with long and short stitches.

2. Split stitch the outline of the cap. Fill the sections of the cap with long and short stitches.

3. Embroider the scales on the cap with 1-strand French knots, using a combination of 1-, 2-, and 3-wrap knots. On the bottom edge of the cap, add 1-wrap French knots.

Blueberry

1. Embroider the leaves with fishbone stitch. Stem stitch the stalk and center leaf veins.

2. Long and short stitch the berries with 1 strand of 3750. Then, straight stitch the highlights on top with 931.

Moss and Grasses

1. Embroider the 2 ovals in the base of moss with turkey rug stitch. Fill the rest of the moss base with 2-strand 3-wrap French knots. Blend 3051, 3011, and 935 to densely fill the area.

2. Cut the turkey rug stitch loops, trimming as desired.

3. Stem stitch the blades of grass alternating 3051, 3011, and 935.

Finishing

Remove any marks from transferring the pattern, then display as desired in the hoop or a frame.

DESIGNERS

CHRISTEN BROWN

Christen is an artist, a designer, an author, and a teacher. She is generous with her talents and considers teaching and writing as an opportunity to pass on these gifts. Christen's design choices, color mastery, and embroidered artistry set her work aside. Each piece is deliberately designed and executed to showcase the components and the techniques she has chosen to incorporate into them. Christen works and teaches out of her home studio in Escondido, California.

Website: christenbrown.com

STELLA CARAMAN

Stella is the creative force behind Why Knot Stitches, a business dedicated to guiding people in discovering the calming and meditative art of hand embroidery. Known for her intricate designs and heartfelt storytelling, Stella combines traditional techniques with a modern aesthetic, creating pieces that inspire connection and mindfulness. Her featured work reflects her passion for crafting meaningful heirlooms that celebrate the beauty of the season and the joy of creativity. Stella believes that embroidery is more than a craft—it's a path to calm the mind and nurture creative freedom. She aims to bring value in people's lives by guiding them to embrace the present moment through the mindful practice of crafting.

Website: WhyKnotStitches.com
YouTube: /WhyKnotStitches
Instagram: @WhyKnotStitches
Facebook: /WhyKnotStitches
Pinterest: /WhyKnotStitches
Etsy: WhyKnotStitches

ALIAKSANDRA DZYACHENKA

Aliaksandra Dzyachenka is a designer of botanical scenes in embroidery. Now she lives in a small town in the Czech Republic, surrounded by mountains and forests. Her creative journey in the free style of embroidery began about five years ago. At that moment of her life, she experienced a personal crisis associated with moving to another country and the birth of her third child. Embroidery allowed her to cope with difficulties and stress and find harmony within herself. Gradually, her recognizable style in embroidery began to take shape, mainly realistic botanical flowers and plants. And she created her own brand AmityFloralEmbroidery. This small business was launched when she realized that she was able and eager to share her flower stories with people, in order to inspire them to engage in their embroidery journey or just to start embroidering.

Instagram: @amity_by
YouTube: /amityfloralembroidery
Etsy: amityfloralembroider

JENNIFER DAVIDSON

Jennifer Davidson of Bloom and Floss is a self-taught embroidery artist who has always been drawn to creative hobbies, but none have brought her as much joy as stitching. She enjoys the mindful, meditative act of stitching, and loves experimenting and learning new techniques. Her style varies, but her favorite designs to create are abstract and full of texture, movement, and color. She sells embroidery patterns for every level of stitchers, as well as finished artwork on Etsy. You can follow Jennifer's creative journey on Instagram.

Instagram: @bloomandfloss
Etsy: bloomandfloss

MELISSA GALBRAITH

Melissa Galbraith is the fiber artist behind MCreativeJ. She was born and raised in the desert of Washington state where her mother instilled a love of making things by hand at an early age. Melissa shares her love of nature through whimsical and modern hand embroidery kits, patterns, workshops, and her books, *How to Embroider Texture* and *Pattern and DIY Embroidered Shoes.* She enjoys seeing makers fall in love with the needle arts, especially that magical ah-ha moment of learning something new.

Website:
mcreativej.com
Instagram:
@mcreativej
YouTube:
/mcreativej

THERESA LAWSON

Loving all things fiber has been a lifelong pursuit of Theresa Lawson. After years of dabbling in various fiber crafts, Theresa discovered and fell in love with how she could use embroidery to create masterpieces from seemingly innocuous materials. Raised in the English town of Bury St. Edmunds, Theresa moved across the world to Seattle. Here she created a portfolio of work and soon became known for her detailed and whimsical embroidered pieces. Fans of her work were particularly taken with her embroidered houses. Now working from her studio on Lummi Island, Washington, Theresa creates embroidered art and patterns inspired by mountains, forests, and wildlife.

Website:
themonsterslounge.com
Instagram:
@themonsterslounge

ANNE OLIVER

Anne Oliver of Lolli and Grace adores vibrant colors and unique textures, infusing that joy into every pattern and kit she creates. With a lifelong passion for drawing, painting, sewing, and stitching, she rediscovered embroidery as the perfect way to transform the colors and textures in her imagination into stunning patterns that embroiderers of all levels love to stitch. In addition to her embroidery hoop patterns and kits, her creations include wool felt ornament patterns and kits that often include the delightful sparkle of beads and sequins. Anne also hosts fun and engaging stitch-alongs throughout the year, where stitchers of all levels come together to create and connect. Join her thriving community on Instagram, TikTok, and Facebook for colorful inspiration and stitching adventures!

Website and blog: lolliandgrace.com
Instagram: @lolliandgrace
TikTok: @lolliandgrace
Facebook: /Lolli-Grace

CARLEY PETTITT

Carley Pettitt (Alberta, Canada) is a self-taught textile artist specializing in hand embroidery. Born in Edmonton and raised on the coast of Vancouver Island, she has always felt close to art and the wildlife around her. Carley uses her embroidery to advocate for endangered species and educate others about wildlife conservation. Implementing both classic and modern embroidery techniques such as silk shading and lace designs, she brings both flora and fauna to life on fabric. By using sustainable and up-cycled supplies to create her art, she hopes to lessen her footprint and make the Earth a better place for the life we create.

Website: nest-embirdery.ca
Instagram: @nest.embirdery

AIMEE RAY

Aimee Ray has been an artist all her life and loves to bring her designs to life in hand embroidery! She is very inspired by nature and animals, especially her three curious kitties. Aimee has written several books of hand embroidery patterns (the Doodle Stitching series) and creates lots of original embroidery and felt sewing patterns and kits. She lives in Northwest Arkansas with her family.

Website: little-dear.com
Instagram: @aimee_littledear

LAURA WASILOWSKI

Laura Wasilowski is a textile artist working with hand-dyed fabrics and threads. She creates pictorial art quilts that are hand-embroidered or machine-quilted. In Laura's latest endeavor, free-form hand embroideries share a similar style with her narrative quilts. Improvised and whimsical, they both express her joy and love of creating art.

Laura's art is collected and exhibited internationally and has appeared in multiple publications since her career began in 1992. She is also the author of five books on creating textile art and an online instructor with Creative Spark. Living in Elgin, Illinois, with her fun-loving husband, she tends her colorful garden when not stitching her colorful fabrics.

Website: laurawasilowski.com
Instagram: @laurawasilowski
Find Laura on Creative Spark Online Learning: creativespark.ctpub.com

LOUISE WATSON

Louise Watson lives in Derbyshire, with her family, in the midlands near the Peak District National Park. The countryside and neighbouring allotments provide a great source of inspiration for all the bright seasonal embroideries Louise stitches. Beginning sewing five years ago, Louise fell in love with embroidery and quickly found her own style within it, creating designs for people to replicate. Louise has written patterns for both Anchor and DMC and is excited to see where embroidery will take her next.

Instagram: @sewbeeeit
Etsy: sewbeeeit
Pinterest: /sewbeeeitembroidery

MEGAN ZANIEWSKI

Megan Zaniewski is a hand embroidery artist and author who has dedicated her craft to capturing the essence of nature with needle and thread since 2013. She is inspired by the outdoors and the time she spends homeschooling her children and learning about the natural world with them. Her book *Stumpwork Embroidery & Thread Painting* (C&T Publishing, 2024) teaches readers how to embroider lifelike, three-dimensional designs that seem to leap from the hoop. Look for her upcoming title, *Stumpwork Studio—Mastering 3-D Embroidery,* in 2026. Megan's work has been featured in art shows, private collections, and publications worldwide, including: Love Embroidery, Textile Artist, Embroidery Magazine, Homespun, Colossal, and The Modern Met. She currently resides in San Antonio, Texas.

Instagram: @megembroiders
Etsy: megembroiders

For a list of other fine books from C&T Publishing, visit our website to view our catalog online.

C&T PUBLISHING, INC.

P.O. Box 1456
Lafayette, CA 94549

Email: ctinfo@ctpub.com
Website: ctpub.com

Tips and Techniques can be found at ctpub.com/quilting-sewing-tips.

Note: Fabrics shown may not be currently available, as fabric manufacturers keep most fabrics in print for only a short time.

CRAFTS/Needlework/Embroidery

Explore embroidery samplers to kickstart your creativity!

Discover twelve amazing designers, eighteen embroidery samplers, and 75+ creative stitches for endless inspiration

Explore embroidery samplers and tips from celebrated embroidery artists Megan Zaniewski, Stella Caraman, Theresa Lawson, Christen Brown, Jennifer Davidson, and more

Includes a complete stitch library with step-by-step tutorials from best-selling author Christen Brown

stashBOOKS®
ctpub.com

11643 **US $24.95 / GBP 19.99**
ISBN-13: 978-1-64403-661-7
52495
9 781644 036617
Also available as an eBook